SHIFT YOUR HOME

THE POWER OF CLOSURE, CLARITY AND CLEARING
TO SHIFT YOUR HEART AND SELL YOUR HOME!

KATE EMMERSON

QUICK SHIFT
PUBLISHING

CONNECT WITH KATE:

If you wish to book Kate to personally SHIFT YOUR HOME or engage her for an inspirational KEYNOTE TALK, please email our team on shift@kate-emmerson.com. To join Kate's private Facebook group for clients only, search for the group LIVE LIGHT LIVE LARGE! Connect with her directly on www.kate-emmerson.com
www.facebook.com/kate-emmerson.page
Twitter: @kate_emmerson
LinkedIn: www.linkedin.com/in/kateemmerson
Instagram: www.instagram.com/quickshiftdeva/

This edition published by QUICK SHIFT PUBLISHING
PO Box 698
Melville
Johannesburg, 2109
South Africa

First published in 2017
2nd Edition 2018
Copyright © Quick Shift Publishing
2017 Text copyright © Kate Emmerson
Cover design by Quick Shift Publishing

All rights reserved. No part of this publication may be reproduced, stored in a retrieval system or transmitted in any form or by any means, electronic, mechanical, photocopying, recording or otherwise, without the prior written permission of the copyright owners.
Publisher: Quick Shift Publishing
Copy editor 1st Edition: Sean Fraser
ISBN: 978-0-620-81937-4

To ENP
Your unwavering support of my journey, right from the start, makes my soul smile. Here's to dancing through life with you, my Argentinian 007. Kx

Table of Contents

Foreword vii
Acknowledgments ix
A game changer xi
About this book xiii
Introduction xv

PART 1 — CLOSURE: The emotional journey1 1
- Amp up your personal responsibility 1
    - DAY 1 – STEP 1: Memorable moments 2
    - DAY 2 - STEP 2: Tough times 18
    - DAY 3 - STEP 3: Soul Sanctuary 20
        - STEP 4: Encapsulate the essence 21
        - STEP 5: Embracing possibility 22
    - DAY 4 - STEP 6: Peaceful warrior 24
        - STEP 7: Sealed with a kiss 25
    - DAY 5 - STEP 8: The ultimate power – CLARITY of intention ... 28
- Speaking directly to the mindset of your ideal buyer 30

PART 2 — CLARITY: Honest assessment 33
- Taking action 33
    - DAY 6 - STEP 9: Ruthless assessment 34

PART 3 — CLEARING: Make it spacious 49
- Clearing up and creating space 49
    - DAY 7 - STEP 10: Live light, live large! 49
- Getting ready for showtime 68
    - DAY 8 - Ready, steady, go! 69
    - DAY 9 - Banish bedroom blues 72
    - DAY 10 - Manky mess or blissful bathroom? 75
    - DAY 11 - Closet and clothing (Part 1) 77
    - DAY 12 - Closet and clothing (Part 2) 82
    - DAY 13 - Refrigerator 'n food 86
    - DAY 14 - Crockery, cutlery and appliances 88

DAY 15 - Books and magazines 91
DAY 16 - Prune your Music 94
DAY 17 - Living large in your living space 96
DAY 18 - Divine dining room 99
DAY 19 - Ditch your dodgy desk 102
DAY 20 - Fling your files (Part 1) 105
DAY 21 - Fling your files (Part 2) 110
DAY 22 - Your choice of indoor section 112
DAY 23 - The final push! 117

PART — 4 SHOWTIME: Selling with grace and ease 119
- Wrapping it up 120
- Your final goodbye 127

Proof and praise for SHIFT YOUR HOME - Life changing stories from real people selling their homes! 129

Other works by Kate 143

Foreword

What I love about Kate's books is that they are scribed in a universal language scripted from real lives – hers and ours. The ink is the blueprint of what really works, of what it takes to live courageously, creatively without clutter. Congratulations on your third book Kate, we are so grateful to be guided to drop it, clean it, clear it, sell it, gift it, ditch, it, and let it go.

Kate is an archetypal Journey Woman; since her seafaring ocean-crossing as a child, she has continued to travel the world. When I met Kate thirty years ago she was about to backpack through places in the East I had never heard of, and just last month she was Whatsapping me from San Francisco. This ability to live her dream across decades has primarily come into being through Kate's own philosophy of Live Light, Live Large. I have always marveled at how Kate is able to move house in a day - untethered by material possessions and mental processes that no longer serve her. More recently she took her approach to the next level and is currently living Location Free – unhindered by a permanent base.

Kate's global travels have been matched in equal proportion by her parallel inward journeys. She has committed her life to personal growth and has traveled to both uncomfortable and exciting places within herself. Her relentless self-honesty and questioning have been more confronting than any guarded border post she has passed through. Kate's passport stamps are matched in equal measure by her self-knowledge; a double treasure indeed.

What makes Kate's outer and inner travels so profound is the generosity with which she takes us with her. Her inspiring way of life invites each person she comes into contact with, to question their lifestyle choices. Kate has made this her life's work; guiding people as they walk through the labyrinthine life-changing process of identifying what no longer serves them.

This work is confronting and challenging, reaching significantly beyond the material realm. Kate's successful approach is both direct and sensitive, punctuated by her glorious laugh.

Natalie Uren, M.A.

Acknowledgments

When I am flying high above the clouds, no matter how long this plane journey happens to be, I have always found it a profound time to look 'down' on life, both mine and others. I'm on a plane flying over the northern ice cap right now, on a loooong haul 15-hour flight between San Francisco and Dubai. Yeah, really, 15 hours, followed by 5 dreary hours in that airport and then another 8-hour flight straight down the African continent to Johannesburg, South Africa. For me, flying means I feel a little detached from it all yet simultaneously totally in tune – removed from life on earth, but at the same time I have a much bigger perspective for all that is, too. I love being on a plane way up high above the clouds – it is *always* sunny up here somewhere on the planet, so I always feel like everything is possible. There are exciting new destinations, hello's and goodbye's, death, life, possibility, creation and dreams coming to fruition.

I am in awe of the process of life and how each and every person crosses my path and vice versa. The last 2.5 years of being 'location free' (considered homeless by some who hear me share this term and squint quizzically in disbelief) have shown me another layer of detachment from 'stuff.' We need so little to be truly happy. Will I have my own place to call home again one day? *Of course!* But for now, I'm footloose and gallivanting globally, sharing my message and bringing forth my work. I could not do that without the love and support of many, many souls – my gorgeous Naldo, who offers me my 'home' when in Johannesburg and is home to my heart and soul. My mum for always being a space-'n-place I can return to for nourishment in all forms – a three-month sojourn in her new home in the UK, or laughing endlessly for a month in Greece together. Big kudos to 'Jemaja,' who always support me and who inspired an aspect of this book when they packed up life in SA. And of course *all* my precious and beloved friends near and far who keep my heart and soul warm. Too many to mention, you know you enrich my life every single day. To Miss Megan, who also loves my beloved Stripes and to my soul sister, NatCat who is always close, no matter where I am.

And then to you, my brave, bold readers and clients around the globe. I honor you in every way! We all need to find a way to serve and find meaning and purpose and I find mine through doing this work – *Live Light, Live Large*! I have deep respect for you allowing me into your life, home and space as you consider this big move ahead; for being open and vulnerable with me and for walking this journey no matter how tough it gets.

For this, my third book, I have to thank all the sacred spaces, places and people that have held me when I wrote, edited, regurgitated and eliminated words along the way. Metz Press for their continued generosity with my books. Sarah, for our special partnership in hosting writing retreats, 'Complete Your Book Mentorship' and 'Pitch to Published Bootcamp'– we are all teachers and students of this pesky thing called 'writing' and becoming an author. It's a wild privilege to bring forth a book.

To every other angel I have not mentioned, you know who you are.

With lightness,
Kate

P.S. December 2018: This second edition of SHIFT YOUR HOME took me to the deepest recesses of my soul as I had to choose, un-choose, re-choose and finally return full circle by re-publishing this edition as a solo author - after almost 3 years of detours. Always be 100% true to your projects that come from your heart and you will never go wrong. You may get distracted by the seductive mask of potential possibility, but you will always come back to the right way.

Now, let's get you started on your life, heart and home!

A game changer

This book is a unique game changer to help you (and your realtor) get speedy results. If you're about to put your home up for sale OR it's been stuck for too many 'Days On Market' (DOM) with zero offers in sight, help is right here. You will shift the usual STRESS & DREAD to feelings of ease, completion and getting excited about selling! Whether you're selling & moving WILLINGLY (upsize, downsize, life-size) OR being FORCED to sell due to external circumstances (death, divorce, relocation, illness, financial), this practical guide offers you a unique approach. You will be guided by Kate to align your heart and home, thus ensuring you're ready to accept your first Offer to Purchase with speed and ease and welcome this Moving Day with less stress and mess.

Here's what **Shift Your Home** delivers:

- Avoid SABOTAGING the effortless sale of your home
- When you have CLARITY about selling, your home will be sold
- Embrace the psychology of CLOSURE and LETTING GO
- Sell your home without SELLING OUT
- Understand the LEGACY of family clutter
- Make empowered decisions on CLEARING SENTIMENTAL STUFF
- Speak directly to the MINDSET of your ideal buyer
- Never underestimate the DISASTROUS IMPACT of clutter
- Never hear the words 'I just didn't like the FEEL' of the house
- Generate tons of CASH by clearing excess stuff no longer needed
- Save TIME and MONEY on packing, storage and removal costs

About this book

It is my suggestion that you follow each exercise chronologically by starting at the beginning and taking it one step at a time. A guideline suggests an ideal pace to follow– what to aim to accomplish on Day 1 or Day 2, for instance – but you may wish to take more time. Many clients have preferred to sit down to tackle all the emotional exercises for closure (see Part 1) in one sitting. That is your call, but remember that commitment requires action, action needs pace, and money likes speed. Each exercise follows chronologically from the one before, and you are guided through the process of how and why to get closure on your home, let go and get ready for show day/appointments. In the process, I offer some lifestyle coaching and generally kick butt. Your butt!

This book will help you to understand the psychology of getting yourself emotionally and mentally ready to sell your home and then making sure your home's look and feel match that clear intention. I have helped thousands of clients – locally and internationally – to clear their clutter, create space and manifest fast, effortless sales through guidance and coaching. You will glean deep insight into what may hold back the sale of your house, understanding the mentality of potential buyers, as well as making sure your home is ready for show day, demanding to be viewed and *bought* by new, prospective buyers! Expect the sale to be fast and know that it's common for sellers to get above asking price. Ready?

Introduction

Irrespective of *why* you are selling your home, it remains one of the most stressful life events for most folk. You feel it in every muscle, every sinew and every cell in your body, I know! The tightening of your solar plexus, the sense of impending doom, the inevitable stress of packing and tearing yourself away from your home. Your nest. Your haven from the world. Your security. And, yes, there may be some positive connotations in moving, and yet it's still stressful.

Perhaps you have been delaying this massive, life-altering decision for a while and have only recently come to terms with what now needs to happen. And now there are myriad things that have to fall into place, one by one before you hand over the keys and take that step into the next phase of your life.

Whether you are selling your home voluntarily or due to circumstances seemingly beyond your control, your biggest job starts internally to align how you feel about saying goodbye with what needs to happen externally to sell. You can ease the process of selling and moving by beginning to think differently – get *yourself* out of the way – and then by making it the most appealing home in your locale at the right price, so that you waste no valuable time sitting around waiting for the right buyer. What do I mean by getting yourself out of the way? Surely it just boils down to a bit of tidying up and appointing the right realtor or estate agent to do the job to earn their commission? Well, no!

I will introduce some unique concepts and exercises designed to help you and all the residents in your home:

- Feel 100% emotionally, mentally and spiritually ready to move on
- Back up your emotional decision with all the right, supportive actions.

Aligning your thoughts, words and intentions with the message you are putting out to the marketplace gives you a real edge when selling your home. Not every part of the process is tangible and I ask you to remain open-minded and at least *try* what I suggest. Take a peek at the rave reviews at the back of the book for added inspiration. If you are selling your home for the wrong reasons or are not yet ready in your heart of hearts to move on from this place you call home, you could unintentionally sabotage the sale. The bottom line is that you may not even know you are doing this because it happens subconsciously.

Once you have decided that you are finally ready to sell your home, whatever your motivation (whether you *want* to sell or perhaps *have* to sell), you will inevitably want it done as quickly and painlessly as possible while still achieving the *highest price possible*. Or better yet, buyers fighting over it thus ensuring higher than asking prices! Agreed? This book is about creating ease and flow around the decision to sell and speeding up the sales process by tackling the task with the right mindset, in the right order and for the right reasons.

Typical scenarios when selling: These are the scenarios that typically unfold during the selling process:

- You make the decision to sell your home
- You consider selling privately to reduce paying agents' commissions - with the internet, it is much easier nowadays
- You might simultaneously contact a local realtor/estate agent to sell your home
- Either you or the realtor/estate agent, gather current evaluations by looking at recent house sales in your area
- Using this information and some market research, you come up with a market-related price
- Depending on where you live, 'home-staging' may be part of your realtor's professional service to accentuate the highlights of your home
- You put your home on the market & wait for it to magically sell

Realistically, the price you want for your home is generally related to several factors:

- The outstanding amount you still owe on your current mortgage/bond
- Other debt you might have that you're hoping to squash with accrued profit from selling your home
- What you originally paid for the property
- The money you have invested in upgrading and maintaining your property over the years
- Your emotional attachment to the house and
- Other personal factors that might come into play

You may even put your house on the market to 'test the waters' and tease the idea of possibility – and then adopt a 'let's just see what happens' attitude. This is never a great idea, because a house sitting on the market and not selling, starts attracting low-ball offers and is deemed less desirable! The question lingers in potential buyer's minds - "why is it not selling, what's wrong with it?"

Sometimes home sellers take the process more seriously, by either offering one realtor/estate agent a sole mandate (which usually elicits higher commitment and energy from them) or appointing multiple realtors/estate agents the opportunity to list the property. After that, the home-owner tends to sit back, confident that their part in the job is now done. In other words, provided your home is 'reasonably' tidy when show day comes along or when potential buyers wish to view and you have dabbed a little fake vanilla essence on the light bulbs (because you heard it helps buyers feel 'at home'), then it's all up to the realtors/agents to earn their commission now, right?

This book is to teach you that *you* are more in control of, and responsible for, the selling process, than you ever thought possible. This means being 100% ready and willing, completing the emotional processes to let go, sprucing up your home and not leaving a single trace of clutter lurking anywhere. Then you will have a home that both looks and feels awesome and you will have buyers making genuine purchase offers in record time.

Don't fall into the typical scenario of abdicating responsibility. My wish for you, is to be actively and honestly involved in the process to disengage and detach from your home to get the sale done and dusted.

This book shares an *easy* step-by-step process that will get you ready for your first show day or viewing appointments in *less than one month.*

So, regardless of whether you are selling your home because you want to move on to the next stage in your life or because circumstances are currently forcing you to do so, your mindset and approach to selling have a profound impact on the final outcome. Can you imagine the joy of receiving your asking price – or above asking price as usually happens with my clients– on your first show day, or selling to the first buyer who comes via appointment? And it *does* happen. Imagine being able to pack up your home with delight and ease because you have already detached, thinned out your possessions, thrown out stuff you no longer love or need, organized all your belongings and are 100% ready to move on?

It *is* absolutely possible, and I am going to help you experience that reality through this process!

It is well known that while your home might have the ideal number of rooms, great space, excellent light, square meters, price, location for a potential buyer – in other words, on paper it's just perfect – they may simply not be interested because 'it did not feel right' to them. If you ask what they mean by that statement, most cannot explain it in logical terms. You see, apart from the physical footprint, the energetic footprint is the one that often has the most significant impact. The energetic footprint is that which you weave into the very fabric of your home and has a staggering effect on the sale of your property. You have to be crystal clear that you are *ready* and willing to leave your home. The notion of 'Well, Kate, my situation is different and you don't understand – I have to sell because XYZ has happened to me' doesn't cut it because that victim mentality and attachment to what *was*, remains an obstacle and will impact the energetic footprint, hindering the speed of and ease with which your home will sell.

When, at last, you are 100% emotionally ready, the next step is to have your home looking and feeling like the best in its price range in your location, making it a no-brainer for potential buyers. Don't kid yourself that the mess, disorder and clutter don't matter – prospective buyers *do* open closets on show days. They really do! No doubt they'll be wondering whether there is enough space for them and all their possessions, but you will also put buyers off if closets are messy and over-filled. Naturally, realtors/estate agents will advise you to clear out, clean up and make your place tidy for show day, but how far do you need to go?

Do this first!
If your home has already been on the market a while, you will probably have already completed this process as a matter of course and can confidently skip to the next step. But if you are just getting started, then ask two to three well-known realtors/estate agents actively selling homes in your area to evaluate your house before you do anything! Before you go any further, call them up and make appointments for their assessment this week. Invite them in to do a thorough property evaluation of what they think the home will fetch on the market and how long it will realistically take to sell given current market conditions. Get their professional opinion regarding any improvements or touch-ups that need obvious attention, to increase its chances at selling fast. If they are not the one who gave you this book, let them know you are currently doing some inner and outer work on the sales process to speed it all up too!

Bear in mind that realtors/estate agents are experts in valuing houses in their areas. Choose realtors/estate agents you have seen performing well, often and recently in your neighborhood. Better yet, get the name of a highly recommended one through your network. Once you have done this, you can continue with the next exercise, knowing they will be evaluating your home later this week. Let's get stuck in with the most vital aspect of this whole process: Part 1 – CLOSURE.

It all hinges on this!

The way the steps and processes are laid out, offer you a guideline as to what should happen when. Some clients choose to do all the emotional closure in Part 1 (Steps 1 – 8), in one go, to dive in deep and fast. Please determine what works best for you, and anyone else involved in this process.

PART 1
CLOSURE: The emotional journey

In this chapter, we look at the following aspects to get you started on your journey of selling your home:

- Amp up your personal responsibility
- Emotional detachment – getting CLOSURE to close the deal
- The ultimate power – CLARITY of intention
- Speaking directly to the MINDSET of your ideal buyer

Amp up your personal responsibility

You know the #1 rule regarding property is always:

LOCATION!

LOCATION!

LOCATION!

But, let's face it after you have bought a house in a particular area, it's location cannot be altered and you are pretty much at the mercy of what transpires around you in the neighborhood and general locale you have chosen. Your home is where your home is, and not a thing in the world can alter that fact at a bricks-and-mortar level.

Your sole aim is thus to get buyers making *signed* offers to purchase on your property at your *ideal (or higher than)* asking price so you can move on with ease and glee, and your buyers are ecstatic at finding a gem of a home at this price after falling in love with this property. Got that?

You need to switch your thinking away from yourself to become focused on the buyers so that they will be yelling...I WANT IT!

Don't fall into the sellers' trap that blames a low offer or slow sale on all the following factors:

- the existing property market
- your neighborhood
- the country at large and government processes at play
- prospective buyers out there
- the administrative tasks involved
- the banks
- your realtor/estate agent
- your mother-in-law (you know how much the world loves to blame them for anything ...)

DAY 1

What you are thinking and feeling and how you get yourself and your home ready, determine how effortlessly you will sell your home. This can be both a scary and liberating thought. If you are truly ready in your heart of hearts and have aligned that intention to reflect outwardly in the physical space, and are willing to be practical within the market, then the sale is yours. It simply cannot be any other way.

Don't do what the majority of sellers do – simply appoint an agent, wake up on show day to put some fresh flowers in a vase, make the beds and hope for the best. This book is about how you can take the right kind of responsibility for getting your home ready to sell in a flash.

Are you ready?

The push 'n pull factors

Before you get to that point where you have made the final decision to sell your home, the multitude of underlying push 'n pull factors will come into play. They need to be acknowledged and resolved in your head and heart first, as this is the real stuff our homes and lives are made of. It's helpful to give them some airtime and acknowledgment.

So why do we tend to delay the heart-and-head decision to sell our homes? We often put off this decision because it means finally addressing and coming to terms with change, which means facing things head on and being honest about them.

Not many humans love change, so that can be pretty tough, can't it?

As you read through all of these possible scenarios below, you might recognize yourself and be nodding along in agreement at what's relevant to your personal life right now. Some aspects may appear at odds with others. Find what is right for you to start the emotional integration and closure at this time.

When working with clients, I sometimes find that just being able to voice the emotions running deep within, can start the dislodging process, inching them closer towards a decision and finally a graceful sale. At the same time, it can often nudge lots of pent-up emotions to the surface that need to be dealt with. Who knew that all this stuff could be lurking beneath making the decision to sell your home? If you feel that any of the points raised here are impeding your progress because they remain unresolved at some level, be sure to get the right emotional support by seeking professional help. Deal?

Some potential, unconscious questions that might be underlying each scenario are offered up for you to contemplate.

Haven and sanctuary
Your home represents everything that makes you feel warm, fuzzy and safe. It is the nest you return to, to find solace, rest, rejuvenation and a sense of wholeness. You heave a sigh of relief as you enter your home, and it is where can be yourself. No one makes too many demands on you here, and you can retreat from the busy-ness of the outside world. No matter how often you go away, this is where you always come back to

land and *be*. This is where your body, mind and soul feel at one, at peace and at ease.

The unconscious question that arises here is – how will I function without this anchor in my life, and will I ever be able to re-create my haven again?

Awesome memories
Your home is where your life has been unfolding and awesome, magical memories have been created in this space. This is where your hopes and dreams were formed, and your life has been lived out here, whether for two years or twenty. Does leaving here mean that these memories will fade into oblivion? What if you can't access all the past delights and happy memories when you are no longer here? The very bricks and mortar reflect your lived life. Your ideals and hopes are ingrained in the very floors you have walked upon. Will everything that happened here just be whisked off with the signing of an offer to purchase, as if they never meant a dime? It can feel shallow and callous to leave it all behind. Will it all get negated now to little more than a faded photograph?

The unconscious question that arises here is - how do I mindfully gather up and move all these awesome memories with me when I hand over the keys?

Healing from all forms of trauma
We may also delay the decision to sell because there is some deep-seated emotional trauma that we might need to work through. While leaving your home in this instance might not be soon enough for you to move beyond this horrendous pain, for others, the thought of leaving may bring all sorts of guilt and regret rising to the surface. Staying might be easier than dealing with those feelings.

You may feel like you 'owe it' to someone to stay in this home. Perhaps you do not feel you have the right to sell it. All these complicated factors might raise psychological issues that need to be dealt with, but – as mentioned earlier – it is vital to look after you and seek support as required. You may have been, or perhaps still are, suffering from physical, emotional, mental or sexual abuse and the resultant trauma in this home.

Whether by a partner, parent or child, violence in all forms is complex and requires professional navigation.

You may also be dealing with the aftermath of external triggers such as your home being broken into, you or someone you love having been beaten or attacked in it, perhaps even left for dead, you may have witnessed a suicide or experienced the death of a loved one within these four walls.

The unconscious question that arises here is – can I experience profound healing and make peace with my decision to move on?

Legacy
If you have children in the family – perhaps born while you were living in this home or even birthed *at* home – what does leaving this home do to them and their sense of safety and belonging? Perhaps they dreamed of living here one day in the future, in their 'family home' passed down through the generations. Perhaps this home was your parents' or grandparents' home and your decision to sell means shifting the entire legacy of your ancestry.

That's a weighty decision to make, isn't it?

Will your family, past, present and future ever understand your current decision to sell this home (and perhaps some of the contents) and be able to forgive you?

Will your children – or even unborn children – ever come to understand? What promises, even if they are implied and not documented, have you made your family that they might expect you to uphold? Is this home somehow part of their perceived inheritance? Tough call!

The unconscious question that arises here is – how do I trust that my decision to shift the legacy of this family home is the right one?

Identity
Our home is where we showcase who we are and how we are faring in the world. It's where we spend most of our money, and for many of us, it becomes the place that represents our 'success' in some form. Notice how you feel when you think of inviting people over for social events; perhaps you are very attached to your barbecue area, or your immaculate garage space, or the chef-like kitchen where you can show off your culinary genius. Or that high-tech home office you love hiding out in. Perhaps it's your extensive library or that spa-like bathroom that makes you feel like a five-star celebrity. What in your home gives you a feeling of identity and belonging?

Is this your castle and can you ever re-create it? Is your home the very best version of yourself and does it somehow also play to your ego, status and identity with the world and how you are potentially seen? None of this is terrible, of course; it's merely about becoming aware that your home is usually tied up with your sense of identity. Your physical address can be something you get very attached to – either positively or negatively. How do you feel about how your home represents the real you? Is your identity visible on the walls and are you aligned in the space, or has your character been out of sync here?

The unconscious question that arises here is – how do I release any attachment my ego-self may have invested in this home to free up this sale?

Comfort zone
Your home is also a place you have come to intimately know; every nook and cranny is familiar to you, embedded in your cells, offering you a security blanket of some kind. It supports and holds your dreams and aspirations and knows your inner secrets. Leaving this home will require something new and different from you. Are you ready for that shift?

The unconscious question that arises here is – am I really willing to challenge the status quo and dislodge my current comfort zone?

Financial freedom
Your life and finances have been bound into the bricks and mortar and, even when a decision to sell is economic, it doesn't just eliminate the emotional component. This move might emanate from a positive or negative financial position. Are you selling this home to shift where your money is invested and create new solutions to improve your financial situation or portfolio for the future? Will the sale of your home free up much-needed cash flow for exciting projects, business, travel and education or perhaps let you breathe by reducing your current obligations in some way?

Or are you being 'pushed' into this sale because you have fallen into financial distress? Perhaps your financial situation has been altered through a recent death, divorce or a business foreclosure and you desperately need the sale of this property to release funds. Perhaps the courts have forced this upon you involuntarily?

The unconscious question that arises here is – how do I align my head and heart with the numbers on the table so that I am ready to receive awesome "offers to purchase?"

Community
Deciding to sell and move also means saying goodbye to your community, one in which you have invested time and energy. Think about the guy who runs the local bar, the owner at the corner shop, the checkout teller who always asks after your dog. The local park that feeds your soul and the gas station at the end of the block that stocks your favorite chocolate en route home. Your neighbor you wave to every morning on your way to work. You don't just say goodbye to a home, you say goodbye to a whole community of people, ideas and camaraderie. Your neighbor has your keys and knows your mother's name. Can you really let go of all of that?

The unconscious question that arises here is – can I uproot and wrench myself away from the safe community this neighborhood has gifted me?

The 'big fat' mistake

Another reason we may feel the push 'n pull effect and put off making big decisions is that we judge ourselves for having made 'mistakes' in the past. Can we trust ourselves to make the right decision to sell now? What if we mess up again? It can be much easier to stay procrastinating on this side of indecision than face how we really feel about our past decision-making abilities. Perhaps purchasing your current home was a huge mistake and has been negatively affecting your circumstances, and you just want to be rid of it and move on already! What if the next move will be your last one – can you afford to mess up?

The unconscious question that arises here is – how do I forgive myself for past mistakes and really trust my decision-making ability now?

Preparing for lifestyle changes

This can cover many aspects in your life that you may be facing and deciding to sell has all sorts of positive and negative ramifications.

Downsizing

Are you contemplating a simpler, lighter and more minimalist way of living? If you no longer want or need the five bedrooms required for a bigger family, or find yourself traveling more for work or retirement fun, is it time to say goodbye to the way you have been living up until now? Saying goodbye to a larger home in favor of downsizing can create anxiety about letting go of the freedom and space you currently enjoy – and that, ironically, could also be trapping you. You have spent so many years building *up* and now you're thinking of pairing *down*?

Are you feeling stressed about how to choose what furniture stays and what goes and where will you fit or store all your belongings in less space? How will you tell your kids that they have to finally collect the boxes and couch that you been storing free of charge since they flew the nest 5 years ago?

Will you need to rent off-site storage space while you adjust to your new, smaller space? It can all feel quite overwhelming, can't it?

What if you make a mistake with your next purchase and go too small and loathe it – it seems all the trend right now, but is it really appropriate for you? Are you downsizing and retiring simultaneously – in other words, is this potentially the last move you will be making in this lifetime? This decision understandably contains so much emotional energy concerning the reality of adjusting to getting older. Sometimes staying put just seems way easier than selling, downsizing and potentially disrupting your life.

The unconscious question that arises here is – how do I field tricky questions from friends and family challenging my decision when I'm not 100% clear about it all yet?

Death or divorce
Are you selling up and moving because recent circumstances have drastically changed and you might be going through a divorce or perhaps grieving the loss of a loved one? It's not fair!

Moving on can feel like it is being forced upon you, that you're wading through sludgy mud, especially if you are making mammoth decisions on your own when you are used to making them as part of a team. Selling this home can be the single most significant decision you have ever had to make and can be completely overwhelming and unsettling. Who are you talking things through with to help get your thoughts in order?

The unconscious question that arises here is – how do I ever work through my grief to gracefully accept this situation when every cell in me is resisting saying goodbye, moving on and starting afresh?

Up-sizing
Perhaps selling this home is linked to expansion and creation - are you starting a family and needing space to grow into? Maybe you're leaving your first bachelor pad, getting married and moving into your first love-shack together? Or making your first foray into a freestanding home to enjoy sub-urban life, close to schools and playgrounds? This can signal the loss of perceived freedom of your current lifestyle and saying goodbye to

an era. It can also mean stepping up to new responsibilities and further financial commitments, which can cause anxiety.

The unconscious question that arises here is – can I manage all the additional responsibility and bills that accompany upsizing?

The empty nest
Similar to the retirement challenge - have all your kids recently left home to get on with their own lives and you are now rattling around this house, hoping for them to appear on the doorstep? Is it finally time to create a new life and home for this new season, this fresh chapter and a lighter way of living? Not having ready-made bedrooms for your family to visit in future can evoke much anxiety, even if anyone seldom visits. Just having the choice can be nice, and selling may mean giving that privilege up once and for all.

The unconscious question that arises here is – can moving home ever fill the void of kids leaving and what if they don't love the new space I choose?

Illness or disease
Perhaps recent changes in your or a loved one's health mean that your current home is no longer suited to you and your needs. Maybe it's too big, too many stairs to climb, way too much to clean; perhaps you now need closets that are easier to pack, level floors with no lips or thresholds or kitchen surfaces adapted for your purpose. For you, selling may mean finally accepting your current circumstances and the potential advancement of a medical condition and being willing to nurture your health going forward.

The unconscious question that arises here is – if I leave this home am I finally succumbing and admitting to the harsh reality of my future, health and what is possible for me going forward?

Emigrating or relocating
Perhaps you are asking bigger questions about where you want to live in the world and why? Selling your home this time around might be signaling

a massive cross-country or global trek requiring a lot of contemplation, planning and trust. Going forward, you will be uprooting everything you know in favor of a potential unknown. It might seem natural to want to delay such a massive undertaking.

The unconscious question that arises here is – can I create an awesome life worth living in another country or will I totally regret this decision?

First home
Perhaps this home was your sign of independence to the world – the first home you owned as a couple, your first bachelor pad, your first home after a divorce. You might be the first person in your family to have ever owned a home, and so choosing to sell elicits all sorts of mixed emotions and, understandably, you might feel an extraordinary connection to the place, one that feels especially hard to detach from.

The unconscious question that arises here is – is now the right time to let go of my first home or should I rather keep this as a potential investment and rent it out?

Once you have recognized yourself in the relevant scenarios above and started becoming more conscious of the underlying questions that might have been sabotaging action, the next step is to get emotionally primed, aligned and ready! Ready to accept that offer to purchase.

So let's move on to the next step ... If getting to this decision to sell took a lot of agonizing, it can be even harder to execute this decision. Even though you may now feel ready in your heart to let go of your home, the reality of the practical *how* is often a much tougher challenge to face.

Your energetic footprint
When you occupy a physical space over time, you are consciously and unconsciously creating a footprint and imprint of yourself (and your family) in every single nook and cranny – moment-by-moment, day-by-day, year-by-year. It is the physical place on the planet where you spend the most time out of every 24 hours (okay, our workplace might be that space

for some of us!) and, more importantly, is most likely your haven or safe space. The opposite might equally be true for you if it has been a place of anguish, heartache, abuse and pain, but that just means your response to that stress will remain locked into your emotional body and within the walls of your home. For the full length of time that you have been on your property and legally calling it yours – whether you are living there or have owned it as an investment and have had tenants renting – you have been adding your emotional, physical, mental and spiritual self to that little piece of earth called 'home'.

Whether you have realized it up until now or not, it is *this* aspect that is the most important to tackle first to detach yourself emotionally from the house, so that you are 100% ready to move on to the next stage.

You will see from Part 1 - Closure, that this is not some airy-fairy esoteric notion; it is filled with highly practical exercises designed for you and the whole family.

Let' calculate it!
Let's say you have lived in or owned your property for just five years. Even if you are a workaholic, you will still probably have spent a minimum of the following in your home:

- 10 hours per day at home (sleeping, eating, living)
  = 70 hours per week

- 15 hours on the weekend (resting, gardening, entertaining)
  = 15 hours per week

- = 85 hours per week physically *in* your home

- 85 hours x 52 weeks in the year
  = 4420 hours per year

- 4420 hours x 5 years = 22 100 hours

- That's a staggering 22 100 hours *in* your home in just five years. For one person only

- That equates to over 916 straight days spent INSIDE this house

Now, that's a lot of LIFE and attachment!

Next, add up how many people live in your home and adjust the calculated figure, to get a more accurate imprint of everyone's energy and attachment to your property.

For example, if there are three people in your family, that's a total of 66 300 hours. That's just hours actually spent *in* the home. Remember that you have simultaneously been emotionally 'plugged-in' to your home the entire time – no wonder there will be a tumult of emotions that need to be considered and acknowledged.

Now think about all the underlying reasons you found in the previous section about why we put off making the decision to sell.

While for many people the list can be endless, here are some typical highs and lows to let go of ...

- This was the first home you bought on your own
- Your children were born while you were living here
- Both your parents passed away while you were living there
- You faced significant life or health challenges while you were living here
- Family gatherings here were filled with joy and delight

Remember when...

- The birthday Aunty got drunk and started exposing family secrets?
- The winter you couldn't afford the heating?
- When your eldest child graduated from college and you took pictures on the front lawn?
- When your only son fell ill with meningitis and nearly died?
- The day your grandchild took it's first baby steps on the porch?

- When Missy had her litter of kittens under the bookshelf?
- The time you started that short running program just to clear your head and then went on to run the marathon?
- All the other positive, negative or dramatic life changes.

All of these become woven in the fabric of your feelings towards the house and entrench you deeper and deeper into the space. No wonder it is so hard for you to consider selling, packing and moving!

It's exhausting, daunting and tough to tackle all of this at every conceivable level for your body, heart and soul.

Now take into account that one of the most important reasons you go to work every day is to earn money every month so that you can buy a home, then furnish it, decorate it, feed yourself in it, feel safe in it, insure it, have a place of refuge, buy *stuff* to fill it, entertain in it, love it and make it feel like a home.

Next, factor in all the countless hours invested with friends, family and pets, or perhaps working from home. *Phew!* Your home is a huge part of your very existence. Yet when it comes to selling it, why do you suddenly think you can just put up a FOR SALE sign and the job is done? No ways!

Your 'energy' is entrenched in and permeates through the very matrix of your home and property, which is why you become so naturally attached to it. It is *yours* and you are defined to some degree by who you are because of it. The same applies to tenants renting the space they live intoo – even though they may not have the final legal rights, for the time they are there it has become theirs. It has become *home*.

No wonder it is so hard to move on … That is why this book teaches you the right way to go about to make it less stressful, arduous, painful and lengthy. The longer you have been living in your home, the more intense and pervasive your footprint tends to be; this needs to be acknowledged and then 'released' before you can move on with grace and ease.

As 'airy-fairy' as this might sound to you, the first step is to let go of the space itself. Think of it as consciously saying 'goodbye' to your home – long before it is even on the market.

By letting go emotionally – of the space and all that it means to you – you are paving the way for an effortless sale. Most people do this the other way around and wait until the very end, when they are packing and readying themselves to leave – and get very distraught when the time comes to say goodbye, as it all just becomes too much. You can now give yourself a chance for a more relaxed, more conscious letting go. Heck, you may even find some joy in the process doing it this way. I have honestly come to *love* moving, because I understand, and have experienced, the value of leaving consciously. By taking all the positive memories with me and disengaging my energy from the space, it means that I leave feeling complete in myself. There is such FREEDOM in doing it in this new, intentional way!

Face it, how many people do you know who love moving home, love leaving any property with joy? Most people (and probably you too) go kicking and screaming, resisting with all their might, hating the packing, loathing actual move day – lending credence to the fact that moving home is noted as a *highly* stressful life event, right up there with the death of a spouse and divorce. Your home is one of the most significant, expensive and sacred purchases you make. Of *course* you're attached to it.

Can you imagine just how cool it would be to do it differently? To *not* buy into the negative perception of moving, or how fast you can actually sell a property by shifting your own perspective? When you are 100% ready to leave and move on, your perfect buyer *will* show up. Eagerly. Approach the process of selling your home from a deceptively simple angle, so you are 100% ready and willing.

So, how do you actually *do* this practically?

If you live alone, do the following exercises by writing all your answers down and then reflecting on them; or perhaps get a dear friend to sit with you while doing them. If you live with others, it is ideal for the whole family to do this together, step by step (children's involvement depends on their age). If more than one person is going to be doing the practical exercises, then I suggest you each contemplate and write your answers down on your own and then share them with each other around the table.

You will be astounded by what you learn about yourself, your home and your family. Enjoy this process.

STEP 1: Memorable moments

We start by focusing on all the fabulous, happy memories that have transpired in your home! You will need some paper (or a big sheet of cardboard) and pen to start creating this smile-inducing list. Write down all the positive, awesome, life-affirming and wonderful memories you have of being in this home. *All of them.* This exercise is designed to bring abounding love, fun and inspiration top of mind. It's about reminding your heart and soul of the abundance of beautiful memories so that you are grinning from ear to ear with delight.

While this task seems simple enough, you need to wander back through the entire time you have lived in this home. It helps to go back to the very beginning; that first day you turned the doorknob and excitedly walked through the front door, just as the moving truck arrived with your furniture and boxes. That moment you took a deep breath and realized you were finally HERE!

How many years ago was that, how old were you and what is the wonderful path you and your family have walked while living in this home? What milestones have you created, goals achieved and dreams realized along the way? Then, slowly work your way up to the present moment. This exercise could take a couple of hours to immerse in the joy and love, and it will be as fulfilling and fun as you allow it to be!

You can also tap into different aspects of your life as triggers for your favorite memories - consider the following life categories:

- Home and family
- Health and fitness
- Recreation and fun
- Faith and spirituality
- Self-development
- Finances and wealth
- Relationships and communication
- Career (including being a full-time mom, dad or charity work)

Inspired by the categories listed above, take some time to ponder the years gone by in this home, looking for all the awesome stuff that transpired here.

Tips

- As you wander down memory lane, you might naturally come across some of the more challenging things and memories that happened too – don't add these to your Awesome list; simply make a note on a separate sheet of paper to remind you of them when we get to Step 2. Please don't get caught up and distracted by these now - stay focused.
- If you are sitting around the dining table with your family, allow each person to complete the exercise first and then share a minimum of the top three memories on their list. Remember, this should be done after each person has written them *all* down on their own.

You have now read loads of information and have started with the releasing exercises – well done for making it this far on your journey. Now you can continue with the next exercise below or wait until tomorrow if you choose …

DAY 2

Today we turn to the more challenging memories, where you bring top of mind the multitude of difficulties, curveballs and life challenges that you experienced in this home. There are a couple of aspects to this section, so please go step by step.

STEP 2: Tough times

Besides drinking plenty of water to help nourish and hydrate your body while you do the following exercises, you may also want to have your favorite meal ready for afterward, or to drink something soothing – hot chocolate or maybe even a glass of wine – whatever you need to support you through this process. In this step, I need you to be willing to dig a little deeper and go a little further. It is often in this step that clients feel like running away, or dismissing the exercises altogether, as it can require a healthy dose of self-honesty to keep going. Acknowledging the tougher times you weathered, is about giving them some airtime to transform them, rather than holding your heart hostage and sentencing you to jail.

1. Start making a new list of all the really tough times, hideous challenges, disappointments and setbacks you've faced while living in this space. Make a list the same way you did in Step 1, starting from when you moved in and working up to present time. You could also use the eight categories listed in Step 1 as potential triggers. If you found any memories naturally surfacing during Step 1, add them to this list today.

2. We don't just want a list of all the tough times and rough stuff you have faced, as there is no point in that, is there? So, now what? Next, I am going to ask you to look with compassion – not in judgment, but with an open heart – at *each and every* challenge, and consider what it taught you or is currently showing you about yourself? Work through each challenge one by one. S L O W L Y. What are the skills or mindset you had to learn, develop or discover to cope with each specific challenge? Somehow, you managed to face it, beat it, shift it or overcome it, and that required something from deep within you! What was it? What can

you own up to and be proud of, regarding how you handled each one?

3. Now you have acknowledged that, can you look deeper to turn it around? Look for the inherent gift, blessing or insight that each challenge revealed to you about your ability to overcome it. It can often help to directly ASK the challenge as if it is a living entity – "Hey, what was your gift to me, or what were you trying to teach me?" Just try it and see what happens. Each of the tough times will hold an insight or gift for you and, you may also find a common thread unfolding.

4. The next step is to project forward in time and imagine using these gifts, blessings or insights to positively impact what you are embarking on now, with the upcoming sale of your home. How can you perhaps tackle it with reduced stress and boosted energy now? Write yourself a little reminder note to keep this top of mind - how every tough time has positive aspects, and you can draw on this in every moment. It's under your belt, in your very cells and will help you sell your home!

To interpret the bigger picture, this exercise requires both honesty and compassion. Make peace with each challenge to gain the insight that been waiting patiently for you. This can appear quite difficult to acknowledge, especially if you need to sell your home due to current difficulties, be that finances, health or emotional distress.

Yes, I am asking you to be bold and courageous. Doing all the emotional work now, upfront, will pave the way for a smooth sale of your home really soon. When complete, share your insights with the others if you are doing this as a family.

At this point, you can either continue to Step 3 or wait till tomorrow to give yourself time to process all that has come up for you. Don't rush ahead just for the sake of it!

DAY 3

Step 3 is a little reward after all your hard work and digging deep - something to make you smile.

STEP 3: Soul sanctuary

I want you to think about your favorite spot in the home; that little nook that is your "go-to" zone, your happy place, your soul sanctuary. This is the spot where you feel the safest, the most loved and where your soul truly feels at peace. We all have areas we deeply resonate with in our homes, yet it is often this little spot that will be unconsciously tugging at your heartstrings making it hard to let go. This has been your place of refuge, safety and replenishment. Is your soul sanctuary …

- Your boudoir-style bedroom?
- The leather couch with plump cushions in front of the TV?
- Your stylish kitchen that brings out your inner chef?
- The wooden bench grandpa made next to the water feature?
- Grandma's dining room table that overlooks the rose garden?
- Your calm, serene bathroom with candles and fluffy towels?
- The quiet meditation spot where no one bothers you?
- Your creative and organized study with your motivational quotes, stationary and art?
- Your hobby zone where you can spend endless hours tinkering away?
- The place you always go to wind down at the end of a tough day and heave a sigh of relief?

Write a page or two about your favorite spot to evoke all the pleasure and delight and ask yourself the following questions:

- Why is this my favorite spot?
- How did it come to be my favorite?

- How has it been so inspirational and of value to me?
- What am I going to miss the most about it and why?

Dig deep as you genuinely connect with your attachment of, and love for, your soul sanctuary. When complete, share this with the others if you are doing this as a family.

STEP 4: Encapsulate the essence

Your next step is to figure out how to capture the positive *essence* of the time you have lived in this home, despite any challenges you faced here. While one all-encompassing word or a short, snappy sentence may instantly come to mind, (much like the title of a great book), finding the essence might also require doing something a little more tangible before you can express it appropriately and wholeheartedly. You could consider the following:

- Create a collage using photographs to capture the essence of this home.
- Create a multi-page scrapbook – each family member could have a page or tackle it according to themes or decades.
- Perhaps you prefer something shorter such as a few simple yet powerful words to capture the essence on a fresh piece of paper.
- Snap a current family photo at the front door of your home to epitomize the years lived there.
- One of my favorite suggestions is to create a Treasure Box. If you are completing the exercise with others, each person could gift one or two precious items that remind him or her specifically of this home. Try some of these ideas:
    - the front-door key
    - a leaf from a sacred tree
    - petals from that rose bush you planted for a celebration
    - a piece of meaningful fabric

- a handful of soil where your pet was buried
- your best scoring school report
- the cork from a bottle of bubbly for a special occasion
- the piece of wood that chipped off the staircase

Remember: *anything goes!* Our goal in this step is to encapsulate the essence and gather your emotional energy. This enables you to take what you need with you as you move, to provide support as you seek closure and let go of the past. Having something tangible to remember your home by is a fabulous way to move on, taking all the precious and positive memories with you. How you choose to do this is up to you, the only proviso is to ensure it encapsulates your home, thus allowing one or two words, pictures or items to connect you deeply to the essence of your home.

As always, either move on to the next exercise or take a breather and wait until tomorrow for Step 5.

STEP 5: Embracing possibility

The next step is to embrace some ideas about what could possibly be in store for you around the corner. This could mean daydreaming a little or even making it up from scratch if you have to – it's all about potential, possibility and ultimately embracing the scary unknown. You may not yet know the next step, or where your next home is going to be. Allow yourself to welcome that critical space between what is no longer appropriate and not yet known. Be comfortable in the 'not-knowing.'

Why is the sale of your home going to be truly good for you? In what way will it impact your life positively? No matter what your current circumstances and whether you are willing to sell and move or feel you are being forced to, can you start seeing beyond the apparent reality of the here and now? Remember that there may well be a lot of stress related to the practical requirements of packing and moving, but this is about finding something beyond that. The following can be useful triggers to start unpacking possibility:

1. I'm excited that ...
2. It's possible I can...
3. This sale is going to unleash ...
4. I'm becoming open to the idea of...

Your musings may uncover something else profound for you:
- I feel ready for a new start
- I am excited to have a bedroom overlooking a canopy of trees
- I'm thrilled to be moving to a new neighborhood
- Finally, I can let go of the pain and find happiness again
- I am so happy to have smaller space to look after
- I can't wait to expand into a bigger family home
- I am relieved I can cut an hour off my daily commute to work
- A new home means better schools for my children
- My partner and I need a fresh start after our financial stress
- This move signals a new phase after my divorce

By seeking out something potentially exciting to step into, you start encouraging your emotional body to let go of the old, thus making way for some space, which in turn will pave the way for the new. You are now 100% ready for Step 6.

DAY 4

It's now time to ease up a little and let yourself off the hook – just a tad. Humans are always making lists in life (either mentally or on Post-It notes) about things they want, things they want to do or more often than not, feel obliged to do every day. Let's make a list that matters.

STEP 6: Peaceful warrior

As we go through the steps below, make a current list of all the points on a fresh, clean sheet of paper, because we will let go – in a practical way – of this list later.

1. I can guarantee there are many things you promised to fix up while living in this home. Here are some ideas clients have shared:

   - Restore the original parquet flooring
   - Resurface the pool
   - Add a water feature in the garden
   - Build a walk-in closet
   - Knock through two rooms to create a larger space
   - Create a spa-like bathroom
   - Re-do the external gutters
   - Clear out the garage - again
   - Put up a garden swing for the kids
   - Hang all your precious artworks

2. How about all the things you promised yourself you would experience while living here?

   - Take that long overdue, overseas holiday
   - Sign up for that local photography course
   - Change career or start your own business
   - Say yes to those sushi classes
   - Throw exciting and elaborate dinner parties
   - Enjoy more downtime at home
   - Revel in more intimate sex after your Tantra classes

This step is designed to finally acknowledge all those things you just never got around to doing and that might now, possibly weigh you down. These unfulfilled ideas and grand plans you never realized can come to represent pain, anger, guilt, resentment or a complete sense of failure at not having lived up to your own darn expectations or commitments. Often life happens - we let life pass us by and time somehow gets the better of us - so you have to be willing to let go of all these lists, to make peace and be a peaceful warrior.

Decide whether any of these items on your list are in actual fact vital, or whether they are holding you back from saying goodbye to your home. Some may still feel appropriate to tackle and tick off, thus bringing much-needed closure and relief to enable you to complete the sale of your home. Or do you need to finally allow yourself to let go of them? Let go of the incompletion of them? Purge the burdensome weight of them? These kinds of obligations naturally drain your energy and make you feel guilty and useless.

Do them, delegate them or ditch them! Either schedule the important ones on your task list or release them once and for all.

Share your lists with the family and then burn them for a real send-off. Make a bonfire and watch these past desires, expectations and obligations transmute into nothing. Repeat to yourself, 'I am willing to let go of all these to make space for the new.' Then start afresh with new decisions to shift you forward rather than hold you back. Let go of the old obligations, that wish list and 'One day when' ... and commit to new goals.

STEP 7: Sealed with a kiss

Now you are inching closer and closer to saying your final goodbye. This step is about pre-empting that and paving the way for your heart. Your home is essentially a living entity that has housed and looked after you through all your trials and celebrations. I would love you to think of this letter as a way to truly honor your home and your time in it – so when you write this goodbye letter, be sure to seal it with a kiss! Yeah, yeah, I know it sounds a little weird, but you have persevered this far and have nothing to lose, other than losing the FOR SALE sign as it is replaced with a SOLD one!

Feel free to use the following format, or create your own that rings true for you. As with the previous steps, each person living in or otherwise attached to the home should write his or her personal letter, and then read it out to everyone else.

Dear ....

(the physical address or name of your home, e.g. Dear 350 Ridge Road; Dear Mount Grace)

I feel so .... to have lived in this space for .... years and I have so many awesome memories such as .... and .... and .... The experiences of people and events in this space were.......................

My all-time favorite memory living here is ....because.. ....

The biggest challenge I faced here is .... and I have learned that I am much stronger and resilient than I thought by understanding .... through the gift and insight from this challenge.

My favorite little spot here has always been... because it makes me feel ....

I am now willing to let go of the fact that I never managed to complete the following things on my "list" ....

....

I feel a bit .... and.................................. at having to say goodbye, and at the same time I know I am ready for ....

I am so excited to move on to .... and I know that someone else can now come in to love you and be held by your precious walls and space. I am ready to say goodbye to you, with appreciation and heartfelt thanks.

Thank you for all the memories, for witnessing so much in my life and for all the ....

With love/Yours truly ....

Place the letter(s) in a special place until the day you move out, then do something significant with them – either put them in the Treasure Box you created back in Step 4 and take them with you, burn them, tear them up or perhaps bury them in the garden.

You will instinctively know the right thing to do for you and your family.

Important to remember
The more you can approach and process all of this with heartfelt honesty and let go of your home emotionally, the easier it will be to take the next step. It also means you will be less of an obstacle or saboteur in the efficient, effortless and speedy sale of your home.

Remember that we are aiming to sell your home with speed, grace and ease, and to be accepting higher than asking offers a.s.a.p.

Now let's get cracking, so you are able to pack that removal truck really, really soon and hand over the keys to your ecstatic new buyer.

DAY 5

Now that you have processed some of the complex emotions and significantly released some attachment to your home, the next step is to be crystal clear on the *how*. Setting your intention is akin to pre-writing the script of how you want the process of selling your home to unfold practically before you. The real trick is to go to the 'end' of the process and write it as if *it has already happened*. Read that again. As if it has already happened.

STEP 8: The ultimate power – CLARITY of intention

Clarity of intention is about sending a very clear message to your conscious and unconscious mind that you are ready to sell with the least resistance possible. It means having absolute clarity and conviction that you *will* sell your home, that you *will* get your asking price, or higher, and that you *are* ready to move on to the next stage in your life.

I suggest you write out your intention in your own handwriting rather than type it out on your computer, and adjust to make it fit your preferred words and language. The idea is that every day when you read it, it gets you into a positive frame of mind that inspires focused action, thus paving the way for the smoothest sale possible.

It's about working with the notion that when I *believe* in it, I will *see* it come about. Do not underestimate the power of this step, even if this concept is new to you – use it to unleash grace and ease.

Remember to write your intention from the perspective of the future, as if it has *already* happened. Use what you feel is appropriate from the following template for your personal situation. It is also excellent to pre-determine the ideal time you wish to be moving into your next home!

Your intention could go something along these lines:

yyyy/mm/dd (date)

I am so happy that moving day has arrived so quickly. After completing all the emotional exercises releasing my attachment to my home, it was so easy to work through all the next steps and my home was sold in record time. People are amazed at the speed with which it unfolded for me. I took great care to honestly assess what needed fixing, sprucing and de-cluttering, so I was really clear about what needed to be done to get it in peak condition for viewings, and in a way that I was attractive to buyers. I was 100% ready to sell and yet still so proud when people walked around the space. Every corner had been freshly spring cleaned, the maintenance work done where necessary, all my clutter cleared and every inch had been thoroughly loved, making it possible for someone to fall in love with it on first sight.

It all happened with such grace, speed and ease. When the buyers walked onto the property, they instantly felt 'at home' and could see themselves living there in a flash. They loved the fresh feeling oozing out of every corner and could see that the house was loved and lived in, but not cluttered. They knew there was ample room for all their possessions, and they knew they wanted to live there from that very first visit.

They could see their dreams coming true in the space by stepping into a lifestyle they aspired to. There was very little that they would need to renovate or change to facilitate the move going ahead. They were so thrilled to be able to move in and start enjoying the beautiful space.

They happily agreed to our price as they were getting more than they bargained for; we signed their Offer to Purchase without any hitches and the sale went through effortlessly.

In the process of getting ready to sell, I was ecstatic to have sorted out every aspect of my possessions and clutter well in advance – this not only altered the look and feel of my home for the buyer but has also made this move a total breeze for ME! Packing was so much easier this time because all the trash had already been thrown out, excess stuff donated or sold; some boxes were even packed in advance, and because everything was already in the right place for show day, the final packing up was easy.

I know that unpacking into my new home will be totally stress-free this time around. This has been a joyful experience and I am ready to move on to an exciting new phase in my life.

Tips

- Alter this letter in any way that feels appropriate, ensuring you are writing it in retrospect as if it has *already* happened. Add or delete whatever you need to make it excite you.
- Once you have written your intention out, place it somewhere visible so that you can read it *daily*– your mirror, desk, purse/wallet or fridge! Get your thoughts and actions aligned into selling mode!

Speaking directly to the mindset of your ideal buyer

You are now ready to adopt the notion that you are merely a 'caretaker' of this space, getting it ready for its new owners. This is when you need to start changing your language as well. Most people refer to the space they live as their 'home' and from now on, I'd like you to think about it as a 'house.' In fact, a 'guest house.'

You are now living in this house only until the buyer moves in, so I'm asking you to consider that the house is no longer yours. Imagine that the place is really and truly sold and your new job is to do whatever it takes to get it in perfect condition for the perfect buyer and get the deal signed.

To step into the mindset of your ideal buyer from this moment on, stop thinking about *you* and *your home*. Everything you do from now on is geared towards getting the outcome you want – for your buyer to sign at your price within your time frame. When you work through the ruthless assessment in the next step, you need to remain detached. This detachment will help you to determine, with honesty, what aspects of the house you need to fix, repair or clean. It also means that at the very least, getting everything organized, cleared of clutter and simplified is not up for negotiation in any way. You will have to do it at some stage before moving, so the sooner, the better.

If ever you notice you are feeling too attached, then perhaps re-read the goodbye letter you wrote in Step 7, and ensure you are reading your handwritten intention from Step 8 *every single day*.

What your buyers want
Your buyers ultimately want three main things:
- They want to buy the *perfect house for them* at the *perfect price* and to move in at the *perfect time*.
- They want to be able to *see themselves living there* (or a tenant living there if it's going to be an investment property). You have to remove your *self* from the house, depersonalize it so that it appeals to *them*! They don't want to see 500 photographs of your family in the house, outrageous colors on the walls, cluttered rooms that leave little space, or broken fixtures that they will have to mend. They want to feel instantly at home: fresh, comfortable, uplifted, inspired and welcomed.
- They want to see the possibility of their dreams and goals coming to fruition in this space. They are *aspiring to a new lifestyle,* and that is what they are really buying – a space that epitomizes their future!

Remove yourself
You have to get yourself out of the way now so they can see themselves living there. Remember that less is more! You want the buyer to heave a sigh of relief at having finally found this home waiting for them and have them jumping up and down shouting:

I WANT IT!

I WANT IT!

I WANT IT!

WHERE DO I SIGN?

PART 2
CLARITY: Honest assessment

In this chapter we are going to be diving deep into your physical home, warts and all. We will look at the following in particular:
- Adopting ruthless objectivity with a detailed home assessment.
- Action for attraction – your repair, cleaning and sprucing plan.

Taking action

Now that you have worked through all the steps to ensure emotional detachment, you can turn your attention to the more practical aspects of the sales process. Depending on which country you reside in, home staging may or may not be applicable as part of the sales process. For instance, in the USA, home staging is mainstream and expected; yet in South Africa, it's only just cottoning on as an idea. If it is included as part of the sales process, then typically your realtor, broker or agent will be of huge assistance in offering the home staging process – perhaps even included in the commission you will pay. It could be a fully inclusive service, they could call in an external consultant that you pay or they may simply make suggestions for improvements to get the space *ready for sale*.

At the end of the day, there is always much debate about how long a recently listed home should sit on the market – Days On Market (DOM) and Cumulative Days On Market (CDOM) – as too many listed days can negatively affect the final sale price. When you finally list your home for sale you want the best possible chance at closing the sale and signing the deal as quickly as possible for all parties involved. Relevant timing in the market is a crucial part of the process for speed and ease. In my experience, there may also be other aspects beneath the surface that need considering in order to ensure that you leave this home in the best condition possible for your buyer. Use your common sense, coupled with your country's norms, and always heed any professional advice from your realtor/estate agent to decide where to spend your time and money as you work through the next practical section.

DAY 6

We now move on to the more practical aspects, by taking a walk around the space and conducting a ruthless assessment of the house and determining how we can take action.

STEP 9: Ruthless assessment

Your next task is to physically walk around your entire property – ideally with an objective friend or a professional contractor – in order to do a proper assessment. If you have a family, or there are a few of you living on the property, you could all do it together, and it is always a great idea to get someone who does not live there to assist you because they will see things with a fresh eye and are likely to be more honest. If you have successfully completed all the emotional detachment exercises, you really should not take it personally if someone tells you something looks horrible, needs painting or looks like a junkyard. Get your head and heart clear before you start – perhaps a short run, a journal entry to pen thoughts or a quick meditation because the sole objective of this exercise is to get the house in tip-top shape to be (professionally) photographed or videoed for show day or viewings, thus freeing you up to take your exciting next step. If you find that you are still experiencing some kind of attachment, you may need to go back and revisit sections of Part 1 again.

So, be brave and tackle this step with ruthless honesty and complete objectivity so you get that SOLD board up faster than you ever dreamt possible.

You are going to rate every thing on a scale of 1 to 10, with 1 being pretty shabby and 10 being awesome. It is entirely your call if you choose to leave certain things just as they are – just bear in mind that those decisions could ultimately cost you both the speed and price of your sale. There are buyers looking for homes to do up and 'flip' and they will want a complete and utter bargain to warrant their time, effort and money in restoring it. If that is what you are aiming for, you may only need to clear the clutter and do the organizational tasks in Part 3, because you will have to move all your stuff anyway and may thus choose to do *none* of the maintenance or sprucing-up jobs. Use your common sense about where to spend your energy and time and keep your ultimate end game top of mind.

So, to repeat, if you are going to go all out, I strongly suggest that you get an honest and straightforward friend to assist you.

YOUR PRACTICAL ACTION LIST TO TAKE CARE OF ALL REPAIRS, CLEANING & SPRUCING

The action list
You need to draw up an action list that will take care of all the repairs, cleaning and sprucing-up needed. If any item on the assessment scores less than a 10, then decide what *specific action* needs to be taken and, most importantly, by what *date* in the near future it needs to be completed by.

You need to schedule those jobs for *yourself*, or appoint a contractor or staff member to get each job done. The aim is to be 100% ready to invite potential buyers though the front door within one month or less from when you started this program.

Set an end date
It really helps to concentrate all your hard work and efforts towards a specific date – the date by when you will be 100% ready for a show day or private viewings to commence. Look back at your intention letter in Step 8 so that you have a fixed date to work towards, and ensuring that the process is short-lived and focused. It can be soul destroying to run a never-ending project that *may* – or may not – finish at some point in the distant future.

A lot of people work on the premise that 'when my house is ready I'll put it on show and advertize it', but it is far better and highly effective to decide the date at the beginning, thus giving you a tangible completion date for your goal. It adds untold energy and positive pressure to finish it all and thus get it SOLD.

It is realistically possible to get everything done and dusted in just 30 days, ready for your show day or viewings and a signed offer. Always keep both your intention and the end goal in mind; this is a new step for you and an exciting beginning for the buyer coming in to love the space you have released from your heart and into the market for them. Remember that this is all about synergy and perfect synchronicity so that just *one* perfect buyer can walk in and say *Yes!*

So, when do you want to put this house up for sale?

Before you take the walk-through assessment, read through the following scenarios and pick one that currently describes you and your home.

SCENARIO 1: Taking a chance
This kind of home usually sells only if it's a *bargain* and the buyer wants to spend time, money and energy to fix it up or 'flip' it.

- The garden consists mostly of dead plants, un-pruned trees and neglected lawn
- The fences and gutters are in need of repair
- Disaster areas lurk everywhere: plaster, plumbing, electrics, structure, perimeter walls
- There are piles of clutter throughout the home and the closets are a mess
- The cars stand in the drive because the garages are filled to capacity with clutter
- The general look is messy, unloved, dirty and run-down

While this house may have some potential, it is clear that it's going to take lots of time and money to get it presentable. This house scores less than 4 in most categories of your assessment.

SCENARIO 2: Everything feels '-ish'!
Being considered middle-of-the-road when it comes to the house and it's potential, could risk meaning that the buyer won't see the full value. This, in turn, means that it probably won't fetch your ideal price and you will have to wait much longer for the right buyer.

- Buyers feel that 'not quite enough' has been done to take care of this home
- The price is considered too high for what's on offer
- The lawn may be green-ish, but it's not well manicured
- Flowerbeds may be weeded but the plants lack any sign of proper care
- Exterior finishes are in average condition with no obvious glaring defects
- Pool is clean, but definitely not sparkling or inviting
- All rooms are fairly tidy, but the closets are stuffed full
- The rooms don't smell radiantly fresh
- The house is fairly clean and neat
- Faults are few and apparently insignificant, but noticeable: some lights don't work, the taps drip and doors squeak
- The paintwork could do with a touch-up: there are scuff marks on the walls and doors
- Outbuildings, sheds, garages, attics and basements seem full and feel cramped and messy

You are in grave danger of getting low-ball offers and this house scores an average of 5–7 on your assessment.

SCENARIO 3: Going for gold and SOLD

This home will have more than one buyer begging to make an offer and you will get your ideal price, or higher in record breaking time!

- You are proud to show everyone your home
- Buyers can view the place immediately because it's constantly show-day ready
- Your home looks and feels like a well-lived-in, highly recommended guesthouse, oozing energy and ambience
- Every inch of the house has been cleaned and spruced up, with evidence of lots of TLC
- Much care has been taken and the perception is that money has been well spent
- Each room and every closet has been cleared of clutter and well organized, showing ample space
- Buyers can instantly see themselves living in this home and thus fulfill their aspirational dreams
- Buyers are immediately aware that there is no need to spend money fixing anything up
- All spaces are aligned and reflect the energy and feel of the house
- There is easy access to all outbuildings and they are clean and organized
- Strategically placed flowers add pizazz and color to the rooms
- All bathrooms are spotless and the plumbing in perfect working order
- The bathrooms feel like a spa – complete with green plants
- The garden is bursting with color and life, and the pool is sparkling aqua
- Carpets and curtains have been steam cleaned, the floors polished and gleaming

- Paintwork has been touched up, re-varnished and buffed where necessary
- The buyers pretty much find it faultless – even if it's not done to their decorating taste – and can't wait to move in.

Buyers want to own this home immediately as it tick all their boxes as the next step up on their aspirational life ladder. This house scores 8–10 in all areas of your assessment!

Remember that you want people to feel expanded, uplifted and happy to be in this home – and then you get to put up the SOLD board!

Of course all three scenarios have their place, so be realistic and don't expect your home to show up as Scenario 1 and be offered the price for Scenario 3! That's just daft, and yet is commonly what many people moan about when selling their home. This is about giving your house the best chance of fetching the best price. Remember that you have nothing to lose by doing the work. It also means you win going forward because when you finally hit moving day, much of your home will already be sorted and even partially packed. Mostly, it is about getting organized, cleaning, and fixing small things that make a big difference. We are not talking major renovations, just routine maintenance and TLC.

You do not want anything negative to make the buyer stop in their tracks and hesitate. People tend to remember what doesn't work, what doesn't look good and how they feel, so don't give them any reason to get hung up on any aspect of this home, because they may wonder what else is lurking beneath what they see on the surface. Any poorly presented aspects, from the front entrance to the linen closet, start raising question marks in their minds. Then they might not trust you – as what you say about the house is different to what you are presenting.

So grab your pen, the assessment list below and your independent accountability partner – who will keep you honest and objective – and go forth with the energy of *ruthless detachment*.

Tip

- Make sure to list a specific action and a date by which something needs to be completed so that there's no messing about or conning yourself about what needs to be done and by when. For each section below, always check firstly the functional working order as well as the aesthetics. Think guesthouse, organized and space so that you think from the mindset of your buyer and first impressions so that your property has minimal DOM (Days on Market).

Home assessment list

Assess each of the following on a scale of 1 to 10, with 1 being really shabby and 10 being awesome and ready TO BE SOLD right now.

ENTRANCE / HOME EXTERIOR	1 – 10	ACTION REQUIRED	DATE
Curb / lawn / seasonal plants			
Entrance gate: paint, hinges, mechanism working properly			
Drive / yard entrance			
Front garden / lawn green and lush			
Sprinkler system operational			
Front flower beds weeded, trimmed, with seasonal flowers			
Garden furniture clean and usable			
Pets' kennels fresh and clean			
Patio / veranda / porch furniture welcoming			
Potted plants freshly mulched			
Swimming pool sparkling, with pump / filter in working order			
Lights / electrics / plumbing in good working order			
ENTRANCE HALL			
Air flows with nothing behind doors			
Floor surfaces clear and accessible			
Hooks for hats / umbrellas tidy			
Hall closet for boots / jackets neat and organized			

Hall table polished and uncluttered			
Photos / artwork straight, clean and photos depersonalized			
Mirrors sparkle and hung straight			
Dumping ground for shopping / purses / laptops neat and organized			
Lights / electrics / plumbing in good working order			
KITCHEN			
Cooking / preparation surfaces 80% free of clutter			
Minimal appliances on top of clean and sparkling surfaces			
Blinds / curtains are clean and working, letting maximum light in			
Stove / refrigerator / microwave working and spotless			
Inside cupboards / pantry neat & organized, showcasing space			
Spices / recipe books – labels / spines face same way for unified look			
Top surfaces of cupboards are clear			
Pets' eating / sleeping area is clean, with blankets washed			
Lights / electrics/ plumbing in good working order			
LIVING ROOM			
Floor surfaces clear and accessible			
Furniture: in good condition and size relative to space			

Books packed neatly on shelves			
CD spines all face same way			
TV / audio systems are organized and wires neatly stored			
DVDs / video games packed away			
Games / toys packed in storage units			
Magazines minimized			
Photographs / photo albums depersonalized			
Artwork clean and hung straight			
Ornaments / sentimental knick-knacks reduced			
Storage spaces organized			
Spaces behind sofas / chairs / doors not hiding stuff			
Lights / electrics in good working order			
DINING ROOM			
Floor surface clear and accessible			
Furniture: in good condition and size relative to space			
Lights / lamps working			
Crockery thinned out			
Glasses clean and neatly stored			
Ornaments totally minimized			
Storage spaces organized			
MASTER BEDROOM (and all other adult bedrooms)			
Floor surface clear and accessible			
Furniture: in good condition and size			

relative to space			
Storage closets are neat and showcase space			
Clothes are neatly hung, with hangers facing the same way			
Clothes are neatly folded on shelves			
Shoes – neatly paired, clean, organized			
Belts / ties / scarves organized			
Bags and purses packed neatly			
Top surfaces of cupboards are clear			
Under bed cleared of all stuff			
Bedside tables minimized			
Kists / trunks cleared			
Books / music / magazines minimized			
Laundry basket empty, smells fresh			
Mirrors sparkling			
Photos minimized			
Artwork clean and hung straight			
KIDS' BEDROOMS			
Floor surface clear and accessible			
Furniture: in good condition and size relative to space			
Storage closets are neat			
Clothes neatly hung, with hangers facing same way			
Clothes neatly folded on shelves			
Shoes – neatly paired, clean and organized			
Toys streamlined and packed into storage units			

Toys on open shelving minimized			
Kists / trunks cleared			
Top surfaces of cupboards are clear			
Under bed cleared of all stuff			
Bedside tables minimized			
Kists / trunks cleared			
Books / music / magazines organized			
Laundry basket empty, smells fresh			
Mirrors sparkling			
Photos minimized			
Artwork clean and hung straight			
OFFICE SPACE			
Floor surface clear and accessible			
All furniture polished			
Storage neat and cleared			
Organized filing system			
Paperwork ordered and stored, showing space in storage units			
Desktop space – surface 80% clear			
Desktop papers / filing trays empty			
Stationary neat – 'like with like'			
All wires neatly out of sight			
Phones / iPods / printer: wires tidy			
Top surfaces of cupboards are clear			
Inside desk drawers are neat - if a potential fixture buyers may open			
Books / music / magazines neatly shelved			
Photos minimized			
Artwork clean and hung straight			

BATHROOMS			
Bath / basin (enamel, taps, silicone) clean and hygienic			
Toilet (flushing, seat, handle) clean and sanitary			
Storage cabinets are neat			
Wall cabinets organized			
Under basin clear			
Bins / toilet brush hygienic			
Tidy-all / hanging units for toiletries			
Shower - grout, drain cover, doors			
Tiles - chipped, grout clean			
GARAGE			
Floor surface clean (no oil, grime, dirt)			
General appearance of space, with items stored vertically on walls			
Garage doors (condition, motor, hinges, remotes)			
Storage space highlighted			
Sufficient hooks for various garden equipment and sporting goods			
Tool storage (hooks, shelves)			
Storage for gardening equipment			
Shelving clean and organized			
Rest of stored goods packed properly (plastic storage units?)			
Ample space for vehicles to park			
All junk minimized			

OTHER STORAGE FACILITIES: loft, basement, garden / work sheds			
Floor surface clean (oil, grime, dirt)			
General appearance			
Doors (condition, working order, hinges)			
Shelving facilities organized			
Packing space			
Junk cleared away			
THROUGHOUT THE HOUSE			
Floors (stains, marks, condition, odors)			
Running boards at base of wall (scuffs, chips, general condition)			
Walls (dirty marks, scuffs, peeling paint, general condition)			
Ceilings (especially around trapdoors and light fixtures)			
Lights (clean, fixed, in working order)			
Light switches (clean and working)			
Curtains (general condition)			
Blinds (general condition, working order, dust free)			
Taps (running properly, closed tightly, no drips)			
Doors (clean, hinges, locks – and correct keys!)			
Alarm system in working order			
Air conditioner / heating system in working order			
EXTERIOR IN GENERAL			
Windows (glass, putty, paint, varnish,			

fittings)			
Entrances (clean, tidy, free of obstruction)			
Steps (chips, cracks, railings)			
Gutters (fixed, cleared, grime-free, not dripping)			
Roof (clean, tiles checked, trees cut back)			
Alarm system, cameras all working			
Drains (clean, work effectively, no odors)			
Plumbing working, no drips			
Bins (clean, neat, odor-free)			
Wood stored neatly			
Chimney swept and usable			

What's next?

It can take guts and courage to be ruthlessly honest and not to take any outsider comments, input or suggestions personally. The reality is though, if you don't do this step thoroughly, you will get low-or-no offers to purchase. Take it on the chin now, and do what needs to be done! Take some time to schedule when you intend completing each of these tasks. Ask your realtor or network for recommendations and then start calling for quotes from appropriate contractors for all those tasks you are unable or unwilling to tackle yourself. Whose responsibility will it be to make sure that you stick to your SELLING deadline?

YOURS!

PART 3
CLEARING: Make it spacious

We now tackle practical ways in which to clear your house of clutter to make it more spacious and thus appeal to buyers who can see themselves settling in here. Part 3 offers you:

- Kate's unique step-by-step process to CLEAR and create SPACE.
- Taking only what you really love and need to your new home.
- Getting a head start on packing to make moving day easy and peaceful.

Clearing up and creating space

Now that you have completed your assessment and have begun scheduling maintenance tasks, it's time to shift gears and get down to the very practical process of clutter clearing and organizing, thus getting ready for show day and viewing appointments. The knock –on effect is that it will also make moving day easier this time around.

DAY 7

If you are working with a home stager, you will still have to do all the de-cluttering and removing of excess 'stuff,' before they can work their final magic to showcase the space and highlight the house's best features.

STEP 10: Live light, live large!
The power of clutter clearing never ceases to amaze me, and stories from clients continually reaffirm the incredible power of letting go to manifest what you want! My strength and expertize is to be able to take you gently through the process without letting you off the hook. You will finally feel the joy of sorting out your physical clutter and creating a streamlined space that will allow you to get that SOLD board put up faster. If ever you feel a little low and find yourself wondering how you are able to carry on

clearing your clutter and everything I throw your way each day, tap into the original intention you created about *why* you are doing this.

To sell your home with ease and grace!

Streamlining your commitment
First of all, let's set the tone for the next steps of this clutter clearing process. If getting organized in your home is typically a challenge (and let's face it, every home needs to be in tip-top shape before people come to view it), then you are going to love the easy-to-follow, step-by-step process. Ideally, you should dedicate at least an hour a day, possibly more. It can also be useful and more effective to dedicate a full weekend to just getting stuck in. Get as many people involved as necessary (including family or staff) to make the process go faster and increase responsibility for the sale of the home with all relevant parties.

I cannot force you to clear out your life, and the mere fact that you have committed to this book will unfortunately not be enough. Yep, you still gotta get off your behind, literally and figuratively, and do what needs to be done! There is no polite or easy way to say it. Focusing on a small area every day will facilitate the process and make it so much easier for you to wade through all your 'stuff.'

Essentially, when we are talking about *clutter clearing*, we are talking about getting rid of all the *clutter* that might be obstructing your home sale. This is how we will get started:

- Unpacking and defining clutter
- Why clear clutter?
- The three categories of clutter
- How does clutter affect you?
- Manifesting the sale of your home

Tips

- Before we go any further, grab yourself a huge glass of water to drink as you continue reading. It can be cold and spruced up with lemon, or hot and jazzed up with some fresh ginger. Off you go ... right now!
- As an ongoing task, make sure you drink 20 oz. of water in the hour you set aside to clearing out each day.

1. Unpacking and defining clutter

When you consider the clutter in your life, and the reason you may have picked up or were given this book in the first place, it is very likely that you are thinking about some of the following concerning shifting your home:

- your upcoming move and the thought of people walking through your space
- your messy desk
- trash that needs clearing
- clothes that don't fit
- clothes you don't wear
- items that are broken
- unwanted gifts stashed in a closet
- things you're hanging onto 'just in case ...'
- old magazines or newspapers piling up somewhere
- that overflowing drawer, closet, room or outbuilding
- too many things in too small a space
- a general lack of organization
- other people's stuff – dead or alive
- sentimental knick-knacks
- baggage – of every variety

While this is a great start and all of these are forms of clutter, we need to delve into it a little deeper. The dictionary definition of clutter is:

- to strew or amass (objects) in a disorderly manner
- a condition of disorderliness
- to make a place untidy and overfilled with objects
- the mess created when too many things are in a place
- a state or condition of confusion

So, while the dictionary version is a great start and does well to *describe* clutter, it does not offer the whole picture. We need to unpack this idea further. For our purposes, we require a more empowering definition. I would like to offer one that sheds some light on the bigger picture, a greater reason, and a better understanding. If we step beyond the obvious, incorporate an understanding of the three aspects of clutter and allow the definition to become a clue to moving beyond its grip, we can define clutter in more accessible terms:

Clutter is anything that no longer serves you, for whatever reason.
Read that definition again. And again. *Clutter is anything that no longer serves you, for whatever reason.* Now ask yourself, 'What does this conjure up for me?'

This definition is all-inclusive, regardless of the shape or form clutter takes. If it is not adding any current value and no longer serving you in some way, it is classified as *clutter!* Cool, huh? Whether we are referring to dated clothes, messy paperwork, limiting beliefs that clutter our mind or congest circulation in our bodies, we can now put all clutter under the same, all-encompassing definition.

Having defined clutter, this now opens up your perspective of what it entails. Even if you feel that you are the neatest, most ordered and organized person, you can start to view your stuff (be it things, people or anything else) with a fresh perspective, and scrutinize it using this broader definition.

Go easy on yourself
This definition also lets you off the hook a little, because at some point your clutter did, and possibly still does, serve you. Perhaps the red dress that once grabbed attention from admirers; the gym equipment you bought and started using to shed those extra kilos; the papers that defined your life; the magazines that you bought in anticipation of inspiring ideas; the knick-knacks and antiques that beautified your home; the stuff you needed to buy when more people lived in your home; the friends who completed your life; the smoking habit you took up to boost your confidence at parties in your twenties; the pain and illness, or even excess weight you manifested to protect yourself; the shopping you did when you struggled to deal with your emotions – all of that somehow served you in the moment, at *that* moment.

So the question, 'Does this serve me now?' is not about judgment, which merely exacerbates how bad you feel about yourself; it is not about whether your clutter is good or bad, valuable or trash, right or wrong, positive or negative, but simply about whether your stuff serves you *now* or not.

It is not about judgment, guilt, shame or blame. It simply means being present and evaluating everything and everyone in your life.

Modern lifestyles
Nowadays there is an incessant and ever-increasing demand on our time, space and energy, and we are constantly being pulled into it, often subconsciously. Our senses are bombarded by a barrage of information and technology, the smallness of the global village and the need to be connected 24/7. Unless we consciously take ourselves off the grid, adopt the concept of reducing, reusing and recycling, and take constructive steps to simplify our lives, the hamster wheel of acquisition will take us on a helter-skelter ride to hell.

So, unless you want to be crushed by your stuff, or your stuff to hamper your sale, it's time to take stock and live with a sense of lightness.

As consumers, we are bombarded with *Buy! Buy! Buy!* The increase in the regularity of shops and businesses offering 'sales' to generate cash flow means that the temptation to buy is ever increasing. We are part of a world of consumerism that encourages purchasing way beyond our needs. Our world facilitates and indeed encourages debt, and promotes acquisitions of every description. This makes it difficult to keep our lives clear, up to date and clutter free. The advent of shopping online has also made it increasingly easy to acquire material goods 24/7 from the comfort of our living rooms, filling the gaps in our emotional lives with stuff.

There is nothing at all wrong with acquiring loads of things, because the flow of abundance, or the joy of buying and spoiling ourselves and loved ones are wonderful aspects of being human – *unless*, of course, it starts interfering with our resources (such as the space we have available physically to store things), or our energy reserves. When it gets to that point, it has already gone too far. Too much clutter can quite literally drain us of all our much-needed energy.

Relative to your requirements is that your clutter will adversely affect the opinion of buyers coming through your home, so it translates directly into staying stuck, not selling – and you not moving on.

2. Why clear clutter?
Letting go makes room for the fresh, the new, the exciting and the endless possibilities that lie ahead in the zone of clutter-free living. It increases our ability to show up and be fully present emotionally, engaged with our lives, as opposed to being pulled down by the weight of those lead-filled bottles. If we look to nature, we see a homeostatic system of flow whereby the natural world always endeavors to regain harmony; nothing in nature is ever stagnant unless it has been interfered with by us humans. Perhaps there is a way we can look to nature to teach us about cycles and the natural ebb and flow that exists no matter what. It may serve us to emulate this aspect of our natural environment, and remember to let things go, to pass stuff on and to thus flow with all the different seasons of life.

We only have to look at the 'external' four seasons to be reminded of when to reap and when to sow. Our lives are very different in winter to summer if we tap into the natural demands of that time. We can also look at the cycles of the moon – since time immemorial, it has been accepted that the two weeks following a full moon is a time for letting go, of ridding yourself of things that no longer serve you. The new moon thus signals a calling of new things into our lives. Nature guides us to let go regularly.

We could also look at our 'internal' seasons – birthdays or anniversaries, for example – which are more in tune with our personal life. The New Year or a religious festival may be a natural pivoting point for letting go. It can also be useful to think of the time just before your birthday as the symbolic season of winter (letting go, shedding and retreat) and getting ready for the growth of spring – a symbolic, personal 'new year' happens on your birthday, a great time to start afresh with the year ahead.

For all you shopaholics reading this, think about the psychology of what retailers are regularly doing by way of their 'sales.' The concept is threefold: firstly, they are tapping into the psychology that you are saving money by buying goods on sale; secondly, that you will feel as if you have missed out if you leave the items there; thirdly, they are traditionally making more space available for newer merchandise. After each season, we see big sales – letting go of the stock they no longer need that is taking up precious space to make space for the new ranges for *you* to buy.

The same principle applies to our daily hygiene when we use face cream, for example. You wash your face first, before putting your cream on. Imagine if, every day, you kept applying cream to your face without first removing the grime of the previous day ... *yuck!* You would look awful, feel awful and probably come out in revolting spots. It would make sense to apply the same logic with every single area of your life too, and yet we battle to do it in our lives, don't we?

Nature constantly reminds us that we should be shifting naturally between different seasons, bowing to the ebb and flow, yet as humans, we tend to get stuck. We keep 'things' for too long and refuse to let go of people, places or habits timeously. We cling on for as long as possible because we're generally scared of change.

Choosing to sell and move home is one of your personal cycles of letting go at a particular time in your life. You are going to be clearing everything in your space so that you release all the old, stagnant energy in your home, freeing you to take the next step. You want every potential buyer who crosses your threshold into your home to feel uplifted and energized, recognizing that there is plenty of space both energetically and physically. You want them to love and connect with the space immediately so that they want to live there!

3. The three categories of clutter
These three areas of life are inextricably linked to each other if we wish to *let go of anything that no longer serves us*. I think of them together as a triangle that either helps or hinders itself. Let's take a closer look.

Physical Clutter
Physical clutter is the tangible 'stuff' we can see, touch and feel in our physical world.

My fascination with how we store and retrieve stuff so that we waste not an ounce of energy or time looking for things, coupled with over 17 years of helping people at a physical level in their homes, has shown me that everyone dreams of living with their own version of order and practical systems. No one feels great about having a physical mess, but all too often people are just too overwhelmed to know where to start – even if you were once the most organized person, life can and often does get in the way.

The physical clutter in our environment carries a lot of weight in our lives (in terms of both actual pounds and the real space that it fills around us). Every time you walk into a cluttered or messy room, sit at your paper-strewn desk or open your closets, you know that your mess and the resultant chaos are stealing precious energy from you.

Physical clutter fills up the actual space in your life, so you do not have to feel or think. It includes clothes, books, CD's, toys, appliances, magazines, tools, car parts, newspapers, documents, food, toiletries and anything else that you can *see*. And yet it has a dire impact on how you *feel*.

Body Clutter
Body clutter is anything that steals your va-va-voom and vitality.

Your body has several internal cleansing mechanisms designed to sweep your system clean. These systems of input and elimination are designed to nourish you and to rid your body of the excess you no longer require (blood circulation, lymphatic system, kidneys, liver, skin, bowels and lungs, for example). If you put the wrong things into your body and do not allow them to be efficiently eliminated, you are physiologically holding onto cellular stuff that no longer serves you. You are literally clogging up space in your body.

Think about excess weight, cellulite, pain, illness, cancerous or other toxic cells, constipation, skin disorders, atherosclerosis – anything that is clogging you up, and stealing your energy and *va-va-voom*.

I am sure you can recall times when you were forced to deal with emotional pain or baggage or perhaps the reaction to walking into your chaotic home yet again, and feeling the way it instantly steals your vital energy and plasters you to the sofa, only just able to flip through the TV channels with not another ounce of energy to spare.

Emotional Clutter
Emotional clutter cannot be seen – we can only experience the insidious effect of everything that keeps us playing small and steals our personal power by lugging around emotional baggage.

This category may seem nebulous to you, but it can be devastating in its negative impact. It is especially relevant regarding all that work you did in Step 1, with the closure exercises. This aspect of clutter takes up emotional, mental and spiritual space in your life, and thus drains or saps your energy, thoughts and time. It jeopardizes your ability to step up and step out in your life, to feel good about your body, to face the mess in your life. It consists of all that *yucky* stuff, such as the negative emotions we cling to: anger, resentment, guilt, betrayal, frustration, hurt, unfinished business, incomplete conversations, unpaid bills, and so much more.

4. How does clutter affect you?
There are seven potential ways that all three forms of clutter can affect you and the effortless, easy and speedy sale of your home.

Direct effect
If your home is filled to the brim with clutter, potential buyers will feel there is a lack of functional storage space, as well as generally feeling it being too small for their needs – and you don't want that! Buyers *will* open closets, and seeing over-stuffed spaces or clutter lurking in every corner, will leave them feeling oppressed, claustrophobic, crowded, stifled and disinterested in your home.

There will also be the general response of 'Mmmmm, I just don't like the feel of the place,' without much more being said. While each potential buyer has their own personal requirements in terms of layout, structure, number of rooms, size, and design etc., take care that you do *not* fall victim to your own mess. Do not allow clutter or a lack of proper, streamlined organization to be *the* off-putting factor, the issue that chases potential sales away, when you have every opportunity to take charge of it.

Remember that we started this book talking about *you* taking full responsibility for the sale of your home?

Unconscious sabotage
This is a *critical* concept! When you have a home full of *stuff* to clear, minimize and throw out as you get closer to moving day, you could be unconsciously sabotaging the entire sales process. Think about this: the sale of your house means that you *have* to get everything organized at some point to pack up and move, right? So can you make the link that,

unconsciously, you might quite relish the idea of the house *not* being sold – just so that you can put off this massive, daunting task? It might require a deep level of self-honesty to be able to acknowledge this, but the aim is to get you *prepared* for your sale and to do everything to unhook any negative charge. After doing all the emotional detachment exercises, it is likely that this is probably no longer an issue for you, but it does make sense to bear it in mind as an underlying procrastination technique.

If your home is disorganized, you signal to the world at large, the realtor/estate agent, yourself and the buyer, that all is *not* 100% aligned. So, quite simply, if you are dreading the packing-up and moving process, why would you want the sale to happen, because that means you will be *forced* to finally tackle it …

Precious time
You waste time every day looking for misplaced things, shuffling piles of paper, running late or worrying about unfinished business, while that 'To do' list lurks in the background screaming at you.

You will also be disrespecting time by never being 100% present in whatever you are doing. Your brain and body are crammed so full that there is little left for anything else. Even though you are physically *at* work, you are non-productive, and do everything slowly, with no enthusiasm, because you feel weighed down or are perhaps hurting deeply about emotional issues so that you are never *present*. You stress about all the stuff you have to do when you get home – and yet, when you get home, you start stressing about all the work you need to do at the office, or the factory, or school. Know that you are doing your spirit a disservice by never being present.

If your *va-va-voom* has up and left, take a moment to think about the time you waste every day by having no systems in place for shopping, housework, chores or effectively handling your email inbox and phone calls. Clutter in all forms robs you of this most precious commodity: *time*.

Consider this: the longer it takes for the sale of your home to go through, the more time you are wasting before the next step can transpire in your life. When clutter is present you are simply procrastinating and wasting time at every level of your life.

Hard-earned money
This issue is multifaceted. Regardless of the reason for selling and moving, financial costs come into play at every turn.

At the most basic level, consider the money you have spent acquiring what you now own in this home. Then you have to allocate funds to keep it all clean (either doing it yourself or paying staff to do it for you); now add the costly insurance of goods, the cost of storing it all (either in your home or, in extreme cases, at off-site storage facilities) and then of course the upcoming high costs of transporting it all when finally relocating. Some people even have to move into bigger and more expensive homes just to accommodate their stuff.

Clutterers commonly buy triplicates of food, toiletries and clothing simply because they have no idea what they already have. And even if they know they have it, they have no idea where it is buried or stuffed. You buy yet *another* black shirt, more sneakers, an extra bottle of chutney to join the four half-filled containers already in the closet, and another can of deodorant. It is often easier to buy another than to look for an item, isn't it?

Every single time I clear out clients' homes getting ready to support them to move, I laugh (with my client of course) when I hear, 'Wow Kate! Now that they're all together I never knew how many tools I had!' Think Tupperware, black shirts, night creams, torches, bottle openers ... you name it. You get the point? The truth is that if you live with clutter, one of the biggest problems I see is not necessarily the amount of stuff that has accumulated over the years, but how inappropriately it is organized and stored.

Emotional clutter also revolves around not being up to date, being disorganized in general, and not facing matters head-on by dealing with them, for example. Think about the real cost of poor financial habits – high interest accrued by paying bills late, losing bills, not invoicing clients on time, fines or additional penalties from late tax submissions every year.

When you wade through all your stuff in preparation for show day and moving day, you will also find hidden money tied up in your neglected belongings or stuff you never use: excessive clothes, books, CDs, exercise equipment, furniture and ornaments. When clients bleat that they cannot afford to pay for professional clutter-clearing services, I remind them that 80% of my clients recoup up to a third of the fee by off-loading their clutter.

Two out of every three clients I see are devaluing one of their most expensive possessions by not being able to park their cars in the garage because the garage is stuffed full!

It is also common, every time you clear up, to find money, both literally or figuratively. People find change and notes in the weirdest places, checks that have never been cashed, receipts that help them claim on tax expenses or missing policies worth money.

People who lug around excess emotional or mental clutter and do not live a clear, light-hearted life will try to fill an emotional hole by shopping, wasting time or gathering things around them that will allow them to feel momentarily uplifted and loved. What they end up doing, however, is spending money instead of spending positive energy on fixing up their lives.

Taking into account what's about to unfold for you, there will be the cost of packing boxes, bubble wrap, packing tape and all the manpower to pack up your possessions. Then there is the transport cost of relocation, and all the unpacking to consider. The less stuff you have to move, the greater the positive impact on the relocation costs.

Sapped energy
You need untold amounts of energy to face selling, packing, moving and unpacking!

Living with any of the three categories of clutter wastes energy, leaving you feeling dull, lethargic and clogged up in the literal sense of the term, and with zero flow of vital energy in your body. Clutter means living in the past and hangs about with its playmate, procrastination. You are being pulled down and held back.

Hiding behind your physical clutter could mean that you are hiding from life, playing small, burying emotional pain and getting stuck in your past. Hiding out behind your body issues – illness, pain, excess weight, eating disorders, guzzling over-the-counter medications – often means saying *no* to life or *no* to opportunities by offering a 'valid excuse': I'm too tired; I have a sore back – you know what I mean!

Your attachment to anything that no longer serves you steals your spiritual energy as you become overly attached to material possessions, which you can't even take with you. We have a warped sense of what is important and allow our belongings to chain us rather than to enhance our lives. It's almost as if we refuse to live mindfully in the present and continue to experience that heavy feeling, one that is nebulous to describe yet tangible to your spirit.

The shame, guilt, fear, resentment, chaos and anger that get tangled up with all forms of clutter simply mean you never allow yourself to be the best version of yourself.

Cramped creativity
When you live with clutter, your thinking is clouded; you have no inspiration and feel so overwhelmed that it becomes impossible to formulate new ideas or creative solutions to your problems.

It is as if you are wearing a blindfold. You cannot see exciting opportunities because all your 'stuff' is blocking the view. Can you remember how fabulous it was the last time you cleared one space, be it your purse, a drawer, your desk, and how it immediately lifted your spirits?

Imagine the profound effect when your entire life is clear.

Procrastination kills creativity because you are always playing catch-up with yourself, never letting yourself off the hook by being up to date. The longer you leave it, the thicker and tighter the blindfold becomes.

Ripped-up reputation
Clutterers tend to be plagued by feeling totally disorganized and unprofessional, and continuously berate themselves. Clutter creates feelings of shame, deep embarrassment and a sense of zero control. There is an energy of 'laziness,' as well as being in 'victim mode,' when clutter is present.

Not having dealt effectively with past issues, not having enough energy or *vooma* to face your life, worrying about too many issues, having too many tasks incomplete and matters unresolved, lead to regularly not 'showing up.' When you consistently show up late for life, social events and meetings, miss deadlines, forget facts, never feel in charge and are always flustered or highly stressed, you give off the wrong vibes. The sad truth is that people judge us – whether we like it or not – on what they first see and experience when they meet us. According to Mike Bova, Vice President of M3P Media LLC, statistics show that first impressions are made in the first 20 seconds, and a bad first impression takes up to an additional 20 contacts to rectify and shift that poor first impression.

The bottom line is that if your clutter is impacting your professional or personal life, then your reputation, career and relationships could be at stake.

An eye-opening way to think about it is to imagine that people – a prospective boss, a promising new client, a potential lover or new best friend – can sneak an all-access peek into your life, both seen and unseen. In other words, they get an unrestricted view into how you live your life.

Now, honestly, would they be dying to meet or hire you, or dying to run a mile?

Your reputation is vital, and your clutter can sabotage the sale of your home. We will systematically work through all your physical clutter. Every single thing suggested, explained and taught will be designed to get you to clear the clutter fast, and get organized and streamlined so that your home feels spacious, light, loved and inviting to your potential buyer to get the SOLD board up!

5. Manifesting the sale of your home

You want to manifest the perfect sale of your home at the right time. I have already suggested reading your intention from Step 8 every day, and it can also help to have a shorter version to work with while you are clearing out stuff.

When you are clearing out the first area assigned to you, simply repeat to yourself:

Today, in order to sell my home with grace and ease, I am letting go of X because it no longer serves me or my life.

Tips

- For this next process, you will need six boxes (or a variety of trash bags) for the actual clutter-clearing process to be more effective.
- It also makes sense, going through the course, to start packing up items you don't need right now. This will simplify the final packing process in preparation for moving day.

Guidelines

Here are some essential tips to guide you through the process.

Other people's clutter

Quite simply, it is *not* your place to work with other people's clutter. If you managed to complete all of Parts 1 and 2, then theoretically everyone should already be on the same page. We get very attached to our clutter, and if you simply go ahead and throw out other people's stuff, you are in essence denying them the process of cleansing and clearing out themselves.

I usually advise clients with teenagers to get real and just leave their chaotic rooms well alone! If their clutter is lying in the common areas of the house, you can ask them to remove it to their personal den, but after that, it is in their territory. Reminding them that they will have to pack it all up soon, makes good sense! However, when you are in the process of selling, and you know your house will have buyers walking through it, you might need to take a different stance. You may find it useful to set some house rules between now and the sale of your home, so that all rooms have the same feel and add value to the vibe of your whole home. Or even consider paying your kids to clear and keep their rooms tidy. Be creative – in other words, think bribes – to reach your outcome.

Can you imagine if 90% of your home is in pristine show-day condition, and then potential buyers walk into the teenage den? If they have children of their own, they *may* be able to see past the mess and chaos, but what if this space is going to be their home office, or a first-time nursery, and they can't even look inside the closets because every inch of the floor is covered and there is no access?

Every room has a function
When in any given space, be vigilant about remembering the overall function of that space. What is its main purpose? Everything you decide to keep in that space, from furniture to knick-knacks to practical items, need to support the main function of that room.

This also helps potential buyers *see* how the space works by painting the picture, so it's easier for them to imagine themselves living in this home.

Every object has a home
What do I mean by this? Ideally, every single item that you own (as far as humanly possible, anyway) has a proper place – its own 'home'. This

allows you to find it easily in the future. Once your entire space has been cleared of clutter, you only ever need to follow one rule: *Once you've used something, simply put it back where it belongs.*

It gets easier and easier once you start noticing when things are not in their rightful place. Its 'home' should be a logical place that allows you to be proactive and efficient in locating it and using it later. At the end of this process, you will automatically know where all of your possessions are. Going forward, it takes not an ounce of time, effort or energy to locate something. You could even be out of your house or office and know 100% where something is located, filed or stored. Of course, this also means that your staff and everyone at home are on the same page as to where something lives. No more excuses.

Like with like
Think about the concept of keeping things 'like with like.' Grouping items together so that they are more ordered in their placement is a very handy way to maintain a clutter-free environment. For example, keep medicines with medicines, linen with linen, and plugs or batteries in the same drawer, stationary and office storage together.

Bear this idea in mind when working through the process. My aim is to create free-space in your head and heart, so you can be doing something far more *fun* and useful with your time, than wasting it on rummaging around looking for things.

Store for retrieval
When you're deciding how to repack items you have chosen to keep, use the 'like with like' rule as a starting point. Then think about where you would most naturally want to look for the item when you think about it. With specific areas, such as clothing, kitchen appliances and toiletries, for example, keep things that you will need most often in the handiest place to reach. And then use the back of closets or spaces higher up, for items you only require every now and then. Or, better yet, pack these items up *now* in preparation for moving day.

No mess morph
Use small wicker, plastic, woven, wooden or cardboard boxes or baskets to keep smaller items together and prevent 'mess morph.'

Loads of smaller containers keep an area tidier for longer, making it easier to place things back in their home.

Music
Sound is an awesome accompaniment to clearing out clutter. If you find one particular area harder to tackle, choose music that will energize and 'funk' up your mood. If the job is more contemplative, such as when you clear out your desk or books, then play more mindful, easygoing music. It can be fun going through lots of your music – and may even help you toss CDs that you will never listen to again!

Bring on the boxes
Before we get stuck into the first physical task, you will need either six boxes and a bin bag (for trash) – or all bags, if you prefer. Allocate them in the following way, with one of the 6 R's:

- **Rubbish:** This is for all the trash, all the stuff you are going to be throwing away – and this bag (or box) really needs to be emptied the moment you have finished an area for the day. Each day!

- **Recycling:** This box is for any items that need to be given to someone else or to charity, to be recycled, or returned to their rightful owner, for instance.

- **Repairs:** This is for any items you are keeping that need fixing, altering or completing in some way.

- **Relocation:** When clearing clutter, you will realize that some items are in their incorrect 'home' – in other words, not their rightful place. Any items that need to live in a different place to the one you are currently clearing out will be placed into this Relocate box. It's much easier to dump them in this box as opposed to getting up and walking elsewhere in your home. To make the process easier, save time and to stay focused, stay in the area you are clearing today.

- **Re-sell:** This is the perfect time and opportunity to generate some cash by selling off items you no longer need. You'll also save money by not lugging them to your next home.
- **Ready-packed:** These boxes are a great way to get a head start on the packing process while tidying up and clearing out. For example, if it is summer you could pack up all your winter clothes (*after* sorting and thinning them out, of course). You could decide to ready-pack the fancy crockery that you love and are keeping, but only use twice a year for big family functions.

Getting ready for showtime!
DAY 8

You have now reached the practical process that needs to be followed, as you start clearing out all your nooks and crannies! Keep the following in mind as you tackle your first project today.

- **Remove:** Remove all the items from within, on top of, behind or around the area you are clearing.
- **Clean:** Do some form of cleaning – even if it is just a quick wipe with a duster or damp cloth.
- **Decide immediately:** As you begin picking up each item to assess what to do with it, handle each item just *once*. Make a decision immediately as to what you need to do with it. There are four questions to use to help you determine your choice:

1. Do I absolutely *love* it?
2. Is it really *useful*?
3. Does it honestly add *energy and value* to my life?
4. Can this be *packed* in preparation for move day?

So think of it like this: if you answer yes to all the questions, simply decide whether the space you are currently working in is the correct home or whether you need to place it in your Relocate box to move elsewhere.

If you love it but can't answer yes to the next two questions of useful and adding energy, what are you really keeping it for? Be honest and ruthless as you evaluate all your possessions, and remember that we are making way for the *new* and *fresh* to come into your life. You want to be inspired to keep things that enhance your current life and are not keeping them because you feel you 'should' be. This process requires you to be brave and to keep in mind what you want to manifest in your life by letting go of things that no longer serve you. It is perfectly safe to let go.

- **Ready-packed:** The fourth question above is designed to get your ready for show day and could be focused around streamlining and preparing ahead of time for moving day.
- **Allocate:** If you are keeping the item, clean it and place it together in a pile to be appropriately repacked or place it in the Repairs, Relocate or Ready-packed box. If it needs to go to someone else, put it in the Recycle box, and of course, throw all the stuff that is deemed trash. It may all seem so obvious to you, I know, but these are just little things to make this process easier for you.
- **Complete:** You have to *complete* an area 100%, and then bin the trash before you can claim that the task for the day is done.

Tip

- Remember the mantra: *In order to sell my home with grace and ease, today I am letting go of X because it no longer serves me or my life.*

Ready, steady, go!

'Nothing is particularly hard if you divide it into small jobs.'
Henry Ford

Hooray! At last we get to today's actual task. I promise that from now on there will be less and less for you to read so that your daily time is spent on your clutter! Each day I will outline the *ideal* versus the *non-ideal* aspect of the space we are working with to highlight it from both positive and negative points of view.

To get you started, we're doing two small areas today: your bedside table and the space under your bed. The reason we are beginning here before we actually tackle the rest of your bedroom is that your bed is the place where you revitalize and replenish your energy every night as you sleep.

Boost your bedside table
Your bedside table is not your local dumping ground. When you open and close your eyes, the space next to you needs to be open and clear and make you feel good inside. It has to lift your spirits immediately, not drain you in any way.

IDEAL: CLEAR AND SIMPLE SPACE Your bedside table should ideally house items you absolutely need when you are in bed. It may hold the *one* book or magazine you are currently reading, your cell phone (not the most ideal place to keep your phone because they emit negative frequencies, but is often necessary nowadays), a lamp, a glass for water and any medication or vitamins you take daily. It may also hold something that lifts your spirits, be it spiritual material, your journal or an object of beauty that inspires you.

Inside your bedside closet or on your pedestal shelves there may also be a few further items used only in the bedroom – perhaps a manicure set, medication, hand creams, hairbrush, or sex aids. This is also where you may want to keep your watch and jewelry if they do not have another home, such as a dressing table or your safe.

NOT IDEAL! Do not keep more than two books next to your bed. These tend to overwhelm the senses and add further pressure, usually making you feel bad, guilty and stressed when you look at the pile of unread material.

Do not keep your cell phone charger next to your bed either, because all the electrical activity is not too good for you – if possible, charge your phone in your study, second bedroom or lounge before you go to bed.

The rule of thumb is to not keep anything next to your bed that is not directly related to sleeping, rejuvenating your body or sex! The area is often a dumping ground for anything that spills from your purse or trouser pockets and becomes a mishmash of little things. Invest in drawer dividers to alleviate losing smaller items you wish to keep here, or a beautiful bowl for loose change, for instance.

Under the bed
The rule is: *Do not store anything under your bed!*

IDEAL: EMPTY SPACE The space under your bed should 100% free of anything! It can't be any simpler than that; sorry, but this is just the way it is because you need the space, airflow and wonderful lightness of energy that comes from a clutter-free space.

NOT IDEAL! Do you *know* how many cobwebs and dust bunnies collect under your bed? Let alone the bugs that just love to sleep close to you and keep you cozy as you sleep!

The only exception is if you have a bed with drawers built into the base set. In this case, make sure you store only linen, pillows and blankets in this space, and today would be the time to tidy that out too. It also goes without saying that anything stored in there is put away clean and ready for use when you need it.

SHOWTIME! Get out of the habit of thinking you can *hide* stuff away – such as at the back of closets, under beds, on tops of closets or any other hidey-holes you have created over the years. It all detracts from the *feel* of your home, the very antithesis of what you are aiming for to entice your perfect buyer!

DAY 9

I *know* you enjoyed waking up in a clearer space this morning and can already feel the tangible benefits of living with just a little less clutter. We are going to stay in your bedroom today (but not your closet just yet – that'll happen later in the week, once you're more into the swing of things).

Banish bedroom blues

Start with your own bedroom – the place where *you* sleep. If there is too much to tackle in one day, simply focus on the 'stickiest' part, the hotspot that bothers you the most and drains all your energy. Begin with something you'll realistically be able to complete within your allocated hour. If you need any pointers, then keep reading – otherwise just get stuck in ...

Using the same formula as yesterday (remember the six boxes) and following the same plan, simply start addressing an area of your bedroom that needs to be addressed, or go for the whole room if you can.

***IDEAL:* YOUR HAVEN AND SANCTUARY** Your bedroom has some essential functions:

- It is where you rest and replenish through sleep
- It rejuvenates, offering you 'me' time
- It is where you dress to perfection for your day
- It is where you attend to your personal hygiene, such as manicures and pedicures
- It is where you read inspirational material
- It is where you connect with loved ones
- It is where you enjoy intimacy with your partner

Your bedroom needs a bed and bedside tables, maybe a lamp or two, possibly some seating, perhaps a dumb valet and anything else that uplifts and adds value to your sleeping space. Some beautifully arranged objects are also appropriate. If you have pets, there may also be a corner for them to share the space, but avoid at all costs their toys and blankets being strewn across the room. We should aim for a 10-minute tidy-up rule.

Today is also the day to turn over or rotate your mattress, and to check the quality of your bed linen, duvets and pillows to see what needs to be replaced. Perhaps take stock and make a note of anything that needs replacing or updating. Once you have completed your bedroom space, you will feel energized, lighter and excited to go to bed tonight.

NOT IDEAL! Your bedroom is not a dumping ground for everything in your life. Even important work-day items such as your briefcase or filo-fax do not belong in your bedroom, so be vigilant. I would also suggest that things such as gym equipment do not belong here. And don't even get me started on having your office in your bedroom! It is bad enough that work infiltrates so much of our time and space due to mobile phones and laptops nowadays, but to allow it to encroach on your intimate bedroom space ... no more! Unless you live in a bedsit that requires the sharing of a small space and what it is used for, try to keep the function of your bedroom very specific.

SHOWTIME! By the end of this process, it should take no more than 10 minutes to tidy any space in your home! When a potential buyer wants to view your space unexpectedly, your stress levels do *not* have to shoot through the roof.

Doors
Do not clutter up the area behind your bedroom door with loads of items hanging up or dumped on the floor. These just obstruct the natural flow of energy. Instead, reassign them to the proper closets. If you have to have items behind your door from a space perspective, then at least hang some of those gorgeous hooks – with only *one* item per hook.

Kists, trunks and chests

If you keep a kist, trunk or chest at the foot of your bed, make sure that it is filled with bedroom-related items, such as linen, towels, blankets or perhaps treasured objects such as photographs. Ensure it is clutter free inside and that its surface does not become a dumping ground.

Move it!

Be mindful not to delay any decisions by simply popping items into the Ready-packed box. Most people make the grave mistake of trying to rush through the simplifying process and delay the ultimate decision of letting go until they get to the new home, promising themselves that they will reconsider as they unpack. In reality, people simply unpack all the boxes into the new closets and never go through the stuff at all. Or, 10 years later, there are still boxes in the garage, waiting to be unpacked or until they call in the professionals like myself. I cannot tell you how many jobs I have done with boxes that are 10 years old and have never been unpacked. Don't be one of these statistics!

Tips

- Always make your bed the moment you get out of it in the morning, or at least after you are showered and dressed. You want to leave your bedroom in a positive state, one that will welcome you back in the evening after a long day out – or your buyer is desperate to come back and view your home at a moment's notice.

- Perhaps most importantly, fill your energy reserves by keeping things beautiful for yourself as you go through the sale process

DAY 10

Are you getting into the swing of things this week? It's fun letting go of all the stuff that no longer serves you, isn't it? Today, let's shift our focus to the bathroom.

Manky mess or blissful bathroom?

When considering your bathroom today, the primary aim is to keep only products and toiletries that are up to date and that you use regularly. Remember the *function* of your bathroom...Yes, yes, I know we're not meant to talk about these things, but let's get real here! Your bathroom is where you do the following:

- let go of the day's dirt and grime
- release internal digestive clutter; and
- get ready for the day in terms of personal hygiene

Its function is a vital part of letting go every day and preparing for the new. So, everything that lives in this space needs to be clean, hygienic and inspiring. I bet you've never even thought of it in this way before.

IDEAL: HEALTH AND HYGIENE All toiletries and medicines kept in the bathroom need to be within their sell-by date and appropriate to your life now. Your bathroom cabinet, the medicine cabinet on the wall, the shelves under the basin and all the other stuff lurking in your bathroom – on the bath, in the shower or in other tidy-all's – are to be assessed today. I personally find that tidy-all storage spaces generally tend to become a 'trash-all' space where you stash anything and everything. Take whatever is not 100% necessary out of the bathroom, and enjoy your open, clearer space. Clean and hygienic are what we're aiming for. Ideally, within your cabinet space, you should keep toiletries on one side and medicinal items on the other, so that when you need to retrieve anything, you immediately know where it is. When organizing your toiletries, I group similar things together, so that I know what I have and don't buy duplicate deodorants or face and body products, for example, and keep them separate, either in different rows or in small organizers such as plastic or wicker baskets. There are plenty of storage items readily available at home or plastic stores nowadays. You may even want to think about creating a medicine box, using something funky and functional to store all your medicines together.

Remember the concept of 'like with like'? This is a great way to sort your medicine:

- stomach/digestive disorders together
- pain/cramp medications together
- emergency first aid (plasters and burn salves) together
- chest and throat medicines together
- alternative or herbal tinctures together

NOT IDEAL! Toiletry products that are more than one-year old need to be tossed. The aim is to get to the stage where you don't have a lot of stock wasted in your cabinets. Do you really need 10 different types of conditioner? Rather rotate and buy fresh, using a better storage and buying system. Old stuff lurking in the back of a cabinet is not good (energetically or hygienically). Toiletries *do* go off and rancid – and what good would that do to for your skin? And sticky bottles and gooey tubes in your bathroom just clog up your energy. *Yuck!*

Remember the clean-as-you-go rule? If you're keeping them, at least wipe them clean, especially the lids, before you place them back on the shelf. If like most people, you have loads of little 'bits' left in the bottom of several jars and bottles, either dump them, gift them, combine them into one bottle or place them out somewhere 'in your face' so you can see them and use them up over the next few days.

SHOWTIME! Create a spa-like atmosphere. Some leafy, green pot plants or a gorgeous orchid add positive vibes to a bathroom. Luxurious, fluffy towels, candles and some mindfully placed *objet d'art* can make your bathroom feel more like a spa – the latest trend in homes that will always add sales appeal to buyers.

Ladies
Ladies ... your make-up! Be sure to assess its age and rancidity – the rule is that mascaras go out-out-out after six months because bacteria can build

up in the brush and cause infections. Make-up also goes off (smell your products!), let alone out of date trend-wise.

Contemplate whether you need to update your look with some new make-up. Perhaps check out a new look for yourself by visiting a Sephora/Bobbi Brown counter or professional make-up artist to get some refresher ideas that will update your look? Be ruthless with the grungy bottom of lipsticks you will never use and old make-up brushes. Make-up should not be more than a year old at most! (I hear your *Eek!*)

Gents
Assess the state of your razors, aftershaves, colognes and brushes, for example, and toss out what is no longer hygienic or appropriate.

Move it!
Why not pack up your 'moving' medicine kit now – just a few items to have at hand in case of an emergency, as well as any regular medication you, family members or pets need to take regularly. You don't want to be stressing about looking for plasters, antiseptic cream, medication or cough mixture in the midst of a move.

DAY 11

Today is the first of two days dedicated entirely to working through your closet and clothes. In my experience with clients, this can be one of the hardest aspects to clear – for guys and gals alike – so you have to approach this from wherever you are at emotionally and take it a step forward from there.

Closet and clothing (Part 1)
We are going to split your closet into two parts – one for today and another for tomorrow. Today will be all about the clothing folded on your shelves, as well as your shoes. Tomorrow we will focus on the hanging clothes. I trust that this will work for you, as it is usually too much to tackle all at once. You may even find that you need to tackle just one small area

of your shelves today, depending on how much you have stored up over the years! Whatever you choose, be sure not to bite off more than you can chew unless you are willing to spend more time on your closet and clothes. It can get worse before it gets better and at some point, it's all going to look terribly overwhelming. Take a deep breath and simply continue, one item at a time.

Shelves and shoes

If you have clothes scattered in more than one room, I suggest you start with your main area of storage, usually in your bedroom. Grab your six boxes and the simple formula again, with one addition when it comes to clothing.

- **Remove:** Remove all the items from your shelves, as well as all your shoes.
- **Clean:** Do some form of cleaning.
- **Decide immediately:** Remember to handle each piece just once and make a decision on the spot. Once again, be sure to answer the four questions to help you decide, but there is also an additional one for clothing.

    Do I absolutely *love* it?

    Is it really *useful*?

    Does it honestly add *energy* and *value* to my life?

    Can this be *ready-packed*? (Pack some of your excess clothing now in preparation for your move.)

    Have I *worn* it in the past 6–12 months? (If not, it's time to be ruthless.)

- **Allocate:** If you are keeping an item, set it aside until you have worked through all your clothing, or place in the Repairs or Relocate box. If it needs to go to someone else, put it in the

Recycle box, and of course, toss all the stuff deemed trash in the Rubbish box.

***IDEAL:* SENSE AND STYLE** You really love and wear everything in your closet within a 6–12-month cycle and it suits your current lifestyle. Your clothes help you make the most out of who you are and accentuate your features. You feel sexy and attractive wearing everything in your closet. Right? Yes, guys, you too!

The reality is that people wear about 20% of their clothes 80% of the time. Be willing to not be one of these statistics. Look realistically at your closet right now and be honest. Come on, I bet that unless you've done ruthless clear-outs on a regular basis, you're pretty darn close to that ratio. What about having fewer clothes that you really love and wearing them more often? Here are a few ideal tips towards reaching the *ideal*:

- Everyone can benefit from your old clothes, so pass them on. Selling old clothes or gifting them to people you know, street kids or charity shops is a great way to make space for some new clothes that really suit you.

- Ideally, you already know your preferred closet style, based on your body shape, personal preferences and what does and does not suit you, and can ruthlessly throw out accordingly.

- If you are not 100% sure, then consider getting rid of old, tired, frumpy and unflattering clothes this weekend, and then perhaps getting some expert advice so that you know exactly what to buy going forward. Both men and women can benefit from this personalized approach so that you have a closet that works for all occasions.

- The rule of thumb is if you have not worn an item in the last six months, or definitely within the last year, it's time for it to go. At the very most, clothes that have not been touched in the previous two years have to go! They really need another home that will love and appreciate them.

- Aim for quality over quantity.

- If you are honest and you have something that you still love that can be altered appropriately so that it becomes wearable, then skip off to a tailor to adjust the item a.s.a.p.

NOT IDEAL! When it comes to your closet, there are plenty of points in today's list:

- Having too many of any one item can be as a result of pure laziness regarding how you shop and not giving any prior thought about what already exists in your closet. Do you *really* need 10 T-shirts in the same color?
- From now on, shop for new clothes only when you are in the right mood. Going shopping with credit cards when you're feeling stressed, down or negative is a surefire way to buy the wrong things for the wrong reasons. Stop buying clothing to fill the emotional clutter hole.
- Keeping clothing just in case? In case of *what*? Get over it – and get rid of it!
- Clothes that no longer fit you? Toss them, and go buy clothes that flatter you as you are *right now*. Stop waiting to lose the weight or until you've developed your six-pack. You will feel so much better about yourself when you wear clothes that fit and flatter you. Give your small or big clothes to someone who can revel in them. (See note on altering items above.)
- Ten pairs of black boots? Those boots were made for walking – let it go, let it go, let it go!
- For hygienic reasons, do not pass on undergarments to anyone else – bin or burn them.
- Consider whether you keep clothes as a crutch. Do they fill some emotional hole for you? Rather ditch the clothes and get real about your feelings; it's much better for your emotional wellbeing, as well as your wallet.

- If you insist on keeping clothes you don't regularly wear, at least ensure that they are stored properly, or the bugs and moths will get to enjoy them, and nature will get rid of them for you!

SHOWTIME! It's guaranteed that while viewers will not open every closet in the home, usually every single bedroom closet *will* be. The sooner you are realistic about and accept that idea, the better.

Organize your closet

For today and tomorrow, you need to consider how you are going to organize all your clothing in a way that works well for you. There are three basic ways to start, so if you need some assistance, simply pick the one that suits your nature and your closet.

1. Organize according to when you will wear it: casual, smart, black tie, gym.
2. Organize like with like: all short-sleeve shirts together, shorts together, jackets together, pants together, slops and sandals together.
3. Organize according to color: all whites together, blacks together, and other colors that you would generally wear together. This last one is a fun, creative way to tackle your closet, especially if you dress according to your mood.

Tip

- Imagine that your closet doesn't have doors and that if anyone walked into your bedroom, you would be proud of the space. If you do not personally pack away your ironed clothes, teach whoever does (your partner or hired help) to work according to your new method.

DAY 12

How great was it to wake up to a clearer room, and open your closet and be welcomed by space and organization?

Closet and clothing (Part 2)

I trust that you have been managing to tackle all the daily areas suggested this week. If you have fallen behind on any of your allotted hours, consider catching up today so that you can start next week up to date. Respecting your commitment to self and honoring your daily hour is about improving your relationship with yourself.

And, talking of commitments, are you still managing your half-gallon of water every day? By now you should be already finding that your skin is clearer, your body feels lighter, and your kidneys are working much more effectively. Go grab your bottle before you tackle the second part of your closet clear-out...

Hanging clothes

Today we tackle your hanging clothes. I won't repeat anything from yesterday, because it's all still valid: simply apply the same information to all your hanging clothes!

***IDEAL:* SPACE TO BREATHE** Make sure that your hanging clothes have space to breathe and hang neatly. If in any doubt as to whether an item is worth keeping, try it on and see how you look and feel in it. If you have lots of belts or ties or both, consider hanging hooks on the inside of the closet door to keep them tidy. You can also buy a scarf or tie holders.

Any special items that you do not often wear, such as dress suits or evening gowns, need to be stored carefully to protect them.

NOT IDEAL! Do not allow your clothes to be squashed up against each other without any space to hang neatly and breathe. Lack of order means you waste time looking for clothes, which means you will be wearing 20% instead of 80% of your clothes.

SHOWTIME! You want to be so proud of your closets that you put a sign on all the doors that read *Open Me!* Imagine how ecstatic your buyer will be on seeing inside your fabulous closets!

DAY 13

How are you doing with all the maintenance and repair work that was highlighted through your ruthless assessment in Part 2? Are cleaning staff, contractors and specialists booked on specific dates so that your show day date happens according to your schedule?

What changes are you experiencing? Take a few moments to think about the past week. What feels better in your space and what looks way better already? Having received feedback from thousands of clients, I can also guess that there is already a knock-on effect in other areas of your life, as you evaluate everything according to the definition, *Clutter is anything that no longer serves me*.

It is now vital to lock into place the concept that as soon as you have clutter-cleared an area, you give yourself every opportunity to *keep it ordered*. Remember that it should only ever take you about 5–10 minutes to clear up any room that has been organized so we can count your entire bedroom and bathroom as on that list now! When things have a home, you no longer have to think about where to put them, and it takes nanoseconds to put something back where you got it from. It becomes the only rule going forward!

Move it!
Before we move ahead to the next task, we need to just take a moment to also check in on those boxes. Are you leaving them to deal with right at the end in one fell swoop, or would you prefer to do it a little at a time? If

the latter is your preference, then today might be a great day to take care of them. Here are some guidelines:

- **Rubbish:** To signal the final end of that task, you have hopefully been throwing out the trash generated from any given area immediately.
- **Recycling:** Choose some items from this box – even if you can't do it all – and get these to wherever you wish to send them. You can also call up some charity shops and they will collect stuff from you. It saves you time and effort. If any of the items belong to someone else, make the call today to organize when they will collect their stuff. Action-ing just one thing will feel fabulous.
- **Repairs:** Take constructive action today – even if it means making a phone call to book in an item for repair, or to actually do it yourself, or plan when to do it.
- **Relocate:** If you haven't already placed these items in their correct home this week, do so today. Walk around your home replacing stuff where it rightfully belongs. Remember the concept that pretty much everything you own has a home. If the place where it needs to live is not yet sorted and clutter-cleared, you can choose to leave it in the Relocate box for now.
- **Re-sell:** How are you going to sell these items? Jumble sale, garage sale, online platforms, Facebook groups, your local shop for antiques, silver and collectibles, auction houses or through people you know?
- **Ready-packed:** When a box is full, seal it properly, place it in a storeroom or storage area for moving day, and make sure it is clearly marked.
- You may also consider **renting off-site storage** for excess stuff if you have too many boxes or furniture, or consider the trendy 'valet storage' for smaller items.

Tips

- When marking the contents of a packed boxed, it is safer to place a number on the box rather than actual contents – for two reasons: it's easy to keep count of the number of boxes you have packed, and secondly, as a safety precaution against possible theft.Removal companies don't need to know what's inside each box.
- Record on a corresponding sheet of paper the contents of the box and where it will live in your new home, such as *Bedroom*. Doing this means that on moving day you don't advertise the contents for all to see. When the boxes are being carried into the new home, you will know that Box #2 is destined for the bedroom. Colored stickers can also help with placing boxes in the right room. Green for kitchen, red for bedroom etc.

Prepare yourself

As you spend time, energy and effort in letting go of more and more things every day, you may already be finding that the inspiration is positively affecting everything else too. How are you feeling this week about getting your home ready to sell? Are you continuously reading your intention from Step 8? Make sure you and everyone else involved in the process stay motivated as to *why* you are doing this, and remain focused on the outcome and the awesome next step you are choosing to take.

This process may be affording you great opportunities for new conversations with how things happen in your home. Be open and willing to let energetic (emotional) clutter start shifting too. It starts occurring organically and naturally. As you clear one area, the next one starts clearing itself out too. Think of it as the powerful, positive, knock-on effect of clutter clearing working its magic in your life.

Great, now we can get onto today's task.

Refrigerator 'n food

Start off with your refrigerator, because this is where food is more likely to be out of date, especially perishables.

***IDEAL*: FRESH AND ENERGIZING** Remove everything from your refrigerator and give the space a clean with some good disinfectant that may be used around food. If in doubt, apply a small amount of dishwashing liquid on a damp cloth. If you can, pull the appliance away from the wall so you can clean underneath and behind it. And while you're at it, clean the very top too! It almost always gets forgotten in anyone's cleaning routine.

- It is vital that your refrigerator is spotless – because this is where much of your nourishment comes from.
- As you go through each item, assess its freshness and expiry date. Discard all outdated products immediately.
- Clean the sticky goo off the top of sauce bottles – that means opening them and cleaning inside the lid too.
- When repacking, place like with like – in other words, all your sauces, jams, and pickles together so that they are easier to find when you need that instant snack.
- Unless it's frozen in the freezer, meat should be stored in the bottom half of the fridge to prevent blood spilling onto and contaminating other food.
- Obviously, religious requirements regarding foodstuffs will override how you store food.
- Your refrigerator is now clean and fresh and smells great! It is well stocked with items that are fresh, healthy and within their expiry date.

NOT IDEAL! Please avoid at all costs:

- old or stale products
- anything past its sell-by date

- 'manky' fruit and veg
- grubby sauce bottles with black, sticky, toxic rims.

Freezer
Go through your freezer and make a note of anything that is nearing its sell-by date that needs to be eaten as soon as possible. You could even make it a household rule that you eat everything in it before you restock.

If you have an older freezer that requires manual defrosting, then this would be the perfect day to do it.

Move it!
Empty your freezer naturally by eating all foodstuffs in the freezer so that it's finished by moving day.

Pantry and food cabinets
As with the refrigerator and freezer, you could make a point of eating and using up most of your foodstuffs before you rush off and replenish them. That is a great inspirational act of spring-cleaning!

IDEAL: FRESH AND ENERGIZING All the same rules for the refrigerator apply here too.

NOT IDEAL! Be vigilant about whether you have overstocked cabinets out of sheer habit, especially when it comes to items you seldom or never use, even if Anthony Bourdain says you should ...

- Make sure foodstuffs such as flours and grains do not have weevils or other bugs.
- Take note of how much junk food or unhealthy options there are in your cupboards. Perhaps you could start thinking about shopping more consciously, because the less junk food (aka body clutter) you have stashed away, the less likely you are to eat it.

SHOWTIME! Remember that buyers will want to see the inside configuration of your cabinets. Ask yourself whether you have enough storage containers for all your items and whether you need to purchase more so that you can make your food cabinet a little more organized and streamlined. Having matching, stackable containers can make storage easier on the eye. Glass is also fabulous for pantry cupboards as you see what's inside at a glance.

Tips

- Always place like with like.
- The items you need or use more often should be stored in an accessible place so you do not have to rummage through the whole cupboard every time.
- The neater and tidier your cabinets, the more likely it is that you will know what is in them, and won't have to buy duplicates unnecessarily.
- You also get shelf extenders – an additional wire rack (ideal for cans) that effectively doubles your shelf space.

DAY 14

Did you enjoy going to your refrigerator this morning and finding a clean, cleared-out space awaiting you? Was there even anything left?

When you are doing your daily tasks, remember that how much you manage to get through in your allotted hour always depends on how much clutter you started with in the first place. Simply do what you can, and let it be unless you specifically want to do extra time in any area. But remember that taking two hours to do something today does not mean you can forego tomorrow's task!

Crockery, cutlery and appliances

Today we stay in the kitchen and focus on your crockery, cutlery and appliances. Chances are you have things lurking in those cabinets and drawers that you never use, and you could dump, sell at your local buy-

and- sell cash-conversion store or even online, recycle or repair so that everything in your kitchen is in *use*.

The exceptions to the 'daily use' rule will be your special second set of crockery or cutlery, if you have one. Just make sure that these are stacked and stored correctly, and that you pack them at the back of your cabinet, so they are not in the way of everyday access to readily used items.

Keep your intention top of mind, by repeating it as you clear out: *In order to get my home ready to sell with grace and ease, today I am letting go of all these kitchens items that no longer serve me.*

IDEAL: LOVED AND USED All your appliances add value to your life and make cooking an easier or more enjoyable experience.

- Your everyday crockery and cutlery are within easy reach, and it is all in good shape. There should be no chips or cracks! If there are, throw them out right away. The energy from damaged goods will sap your own, never mind the germs that lurk in the cracks ...
- Remember the all-important formula you used for your closet and implement it ruthlessly in the kitchen, adding an additional evaluation question:
- Do I absolutely *love* it?
- Is it really *useful*?
- Does it honestly add *energy* and *value* to my life?
- Can I *ready-pack* this?
- Have I used this in the past six months?
- Does it have any chips or cracks?
- Take a good look at your countertops. Is there too much stuff lurking there and do you need to store some of it away in the cupboards to simplify the space again? When you walk into your kitchen, it should feel clean, airy and light, with heaps of space to prepare food.

NOT IDEAL! Do not be tempted to hang on to gadgets and other supposedly 'useful' appliances that never see the light of day. As with clothing, if you have not used it in the last six months, then why would you start now? Get rid of them, donate them, or better yet, sell them for cash.

- I'm afraid that even if you answered *Yes* to the first evaluation questions, when it comes to things that you cook in, eat off or eat with, there is *no* room for chips and cracks. They are a breeding ground for bacteria. Let them go! You may have to wait a week or two till payday to replace a broken pot, but at least make a note that it must go as soon as possible.

- Obey the 80/20 rule: 80% of your countertop is clutter free, thus freeing up space on which to work. Most households get lazy about putting stuff away and has 80% of the area filled with clutter. Be ruthless.

- Keeping lots of mismatched items from different sets can be very draining. Unless you are into the eclectic look or boast an impressive collection of vintage or antique pieces and genuinely love the quirkiness they offer, then perhaps you've been hanging on to them long enough. Get rid of them and buy one new, complete set that you love. Gift the mismatched ones to a community center or charity, and let someone else who is just starting out in their own apartment, such as a student, enjoy them. Remember that you are making room for the new to come whizzing into your life.

SHOWTIME! To keep your countertops neat and tidy, why not enjoy one mindfully placed item such as a beautiful bowl or an interesting tray in the spot where you usually dump anything that you need to as you step into your kitchen. So often we enter the kitchen first when we come home (we need a cup of tea, it's connected to our garage, or we are carrying shopping in from the garage). If items such as mail, cell phones, purse, keys or diary, for instance, don't have a specific storage place, you will dump them anywhere and then waste time looking for them later. Perhaps this is one bad habit that you can let go of by implementing a new way? Create a 'hotspot' that is designed to collect all these things you usually leave lying around; that way you will always know exactly where they are to retrieve them. But remember, too, to keep an eye on your hotspot, bearing in mind show day and buyers! Relocate stuff back to its real 'home' weekly.

DAY 15

While clutter clearing can be a tough job physically and an even tougher one emotionally, it is still mandatory to have some FUN with this process of letting go. Right at the beginning of this process do you remember I suggested that music was a FANTASTIC accompaniment to clutter clearing? If you have not used it at all, why not try it today and it will be a heads-up and lead perfectly into tomorrow's task anyway!!

Books and magazines

Everyone has a different relationship with books – for some, they are purely for pleasure, for others reference works, others collect specific topics or genres or it may be a personal dream to have an entire library. There are no right or wrongs, other than that you love what you keep. All the same rules apply.

IDEAL: LOVE THE BOOKS YOU OWN Books can feed your soul – or can also simply be lumps of old paper, collecting dust. Nowadays, with the advent of online e-books and audio books, you may choose not to have as many physical books in your possession – I recently did a mammoth clear-out of journals and books, thus clearing another layer in an already minimalist life. It was all part of my 2016/17 year to become *location free*. I let go of all but four books, including many gifted to me by the authors themselves. Now, when I need to locate information about a topic, I still manage to track it down, but I do not have to necessarily *own* it anymore. Books might, on the other hand, be a no-go zone for you; if so, then all I challenge you to, is that you be one of those people who adore all the books you have and keep nothing out of obligation.

- If you are a serious book collector, today's task might be a slightly different one for you, because your books may have a lot of sentimental *and* monetary value. If this is your situation, thentoday could be about cleaning and packing at least *some* of them up, simply so that you can get ready for moving day.

- Just consider that if you have too many books that are threatening to overtake some space, it may prove too overwhelming for a prospective buyer – remember that you are the custodian of the space and need to think of it as a guesthouse, getting it show-day ready. So make sure any books that are going to be on show are interestingly displayed, and free of dust.

- Books are living things that love being used and read. Is a book even a book if it is never opened and read, or allowed to pass on its wisdom to you?

- Ensure that you clean your books as you are going through them because dust and mold can damage them – dust brings bugs and mold can irreparably damage paper.

- Keep the books you wish to, and relegate the others to one of your boxes, but I would never suggest throwing any books away – there is *always* someone needing books. Here are some other places that might welcome your books:

    - schools (to help build their libraries)
    - your town library
    - local colleges or universities
    - retirement homes
    - hospices
    - churches
    - book clubs
    - doctors' surgeries
    - charity shops that could sell them to raise funds

- friends who appreciate the books you love too
- a corporate library (if relevant to that business)

NOT IDEAL! If you have gathered lots of other people's books, place them in your Recycle box and get them back to their owners. The same goes for the books that you have lent to someone. If they are prized books that you hold dear, get them back, because their absence can lead to some of that energetic clutter – in other words, represent loose threads in your life. If something is owed to you, then get it back.

- Don't keep books out of guilt – who does that serve?
- Do not keep every novel you have ever read … Move on from Danielle Steele and Tom Clancy.

SHOWTIME! To prepare for show day, organize your books according to whatever works for you: size, category, area of your life or even color, for instance. You could also place some of your favorite books out on display on your coffee table, so you are more likely to utilize them. Most of all, they need to be appreciated.

Magazines

I bet you also have piles of magazines lurking in some unsuspected corner of a room? Magazines tend to represent the promise of tasty treats you'll conjure up one day, exotic holidays, inspirational articles, financial acumen and staying abreast of your industry news – we all tend to keep a few just in case. Or more than a few! Today is a great day to be ruthless, applying the same rules as for books. If you really want to keep that recipe (and intend to use it), tear it out and file it in a lever-arch and store it in sight in the kitchen. If you are genuinely a devoted gardener, then why not create a *Gardening tips* folder or start your travel-destination vision board. Hospitals, clinics, libraries and schools will gladly take your unwanted magazines. As a rule of thumb, unless you are making them an aesthetic statement of art in a particular space, I suggest you do not keep any magazines beyond a year.

Move it!
I simply *love* second-hand bookshops! They will take your old books – some also take CD's and DVD's – and give you cash for them or they give you store credit to buy more books of your choice. What a cool win-win situation.

DAY 16

When you cleared out your books and magazines yesterday, I suggested using music to enhance your experience and hinted that it would lead to today's task. In fact, you might have already started clearing it all out ...

Prune your Music
Just as it is with our books, we can get very attached to music. But if we never go through it all and assess whether this is still something we enjoy now, the CD collection simply expands and gets out of control, year after year. And yet we never listen to a quarter of it! The same rule we applied to clothing, applies here – we listen to 20% of our music 80% of the time. Maybe it's time to shift that percentage?

Nowadays, most people store their music on iPads and iPods, and sometimes even on CDs. Some of you may still be using tapes or even LPs. Today is for sorting through wherever you personally store your music.

IDEAL: THE FIVE-SECOND RULE The real test is - are you able to locate any music you want to play, in five seconds?

- Ideally, your music should be well categorized in a way that works for you, be it via category or alphabetically.
- You love every artist and album that you own, listening to it at least once every 6–12 months (the same as the clothing rule).
- After you have removed all your CDs from where they are stored and have given the space a wipe, start sifting through what you own and be honest with yourself: Do I listen to this? Will I ever listen to it again?

- Check that your CDs are in the right cases – there is nothing worse than finding the cover you want, only to be confronted with a different CD inside.
- Think about recycling unwanted CDs by selling them to a second-hand shop for cash or credit to put towards music you would love to own now. Alternatively, you can also gift music to friends you know would appreciate it or transfer them all to an MP3 format so you can have all your music in your car, for example.
- Because our music system is usually an integral part of our living area and this is a communal and frequently used area, it might be cool to get your partner or kids to help you.

NOT IDEAL! Don't be tempted to keep music because you're just too lazy to go through it and make courageous decisions about what you need in your life right now.

SHOWTIME! Consider what music to play when you have potential buyers coming to look at your home. Playing appropriate music will help them connect more emotionally to the space as they walk in for the first time. This is a massive advantage of having a realtor/estate agent and an appointment for viewing, as you will be able to glean information about them before they enter your space. Remember the concept of playing to the *mindset* of your buyer

iPods and MP3's
Double check all your downloads and streamline what you have saved. Ensure that you have appropriate back-ups so that it is all in perfect order. There is nothing worse than losing everything stored on that nifty gadget, so rather be prepared for an unexpected loss of music – because it *can* happen.

Storage
When you have decided what music you are definitely keeping, you need to start asking whether there is a better system of storage or organization

than the one you have been using. Think about how you want to retrieve them?

While MP3s and iTunes do it all for you, the same isn't true for hard copies. The less you have to think about where each CD is located, the less time and effort it will take you in future to find the one you want to listen to, and you'll also know where to place it in its proper 'home' once you have listened to it. Make sense?

The most popular ways in which to store music are:

- Alphabetically – either by first or last name of the artist or the group.
- Types or genres of music – classical, jazz, rock and modern.
- By each decade
- According to how often you listen to them. So your favorites, the ones you always play, could be kept together, with less-used ones separate from them.

DAY 17

Today is the day we move onto the bigger rooms in your home at last!

Living large in your living space

Your living area is your open, social space, the one you share with family, entertain guests, replenish at the end of the day and where you read, relax or party up a storm.

IDEAL: A REFLECTION OF YOUR PERSONALITY In many ways, this space is the center of your home and is ideally a beautiful haven that energizes you when you walk into it. It will have both functional pieces (sofas and a coffee table) and aesthetic pieces (art, vases, candles, treasures) that all work together to create the amazing space you want.

- Generally, you'll want to create some beautiful focal points. This does not mean that every tabletop has to be crammed full. Make sure that the hour you spend today will leave your living area clearer, fresher and with at least a little more space. Read through the ideas below, pick what matters most to you, and get stuck in.
- Your living area usually involves bigger tasks such as books, photos and CD's, which is why we tackled these over the past two days – so that we have a head start on the bigger space.
- When clearing your living area, you may want to shift furniture around for a new look that will instantly refresh the feel of the room and offer you a new perspective.
- If you have plants, check whether they need repotting into bigger pots so they can breathe and grow again. Remove all the dead parts and even give the leaves a wipe. Yes, odd I know, but the leaves of indoor plants gather dust and then they can't breathe. It all just adds gravitas to the idea that you have looked after and taken care of everything in this home. It fosters trust in the buyer – and quite frankly your home deserves this level of TLC from you.
- If you live with pets, make sure their toys, blankets and baskets are arranged neatly in one area rather than scattered chaotically. The same applies to the kids' stuff: keep handy (and in style relevant to the adult living space) storage boxes where all their toys can be tossed in three minutes flat. Teach young children to help you with this task and, as they grow older allow them to put toys away on their own. You could even make a game of it. If you always do it, you will always do it!
- Think about what you can let go of to lighten up your living space. Depending on where your front door is situated, you may want to place some nice coat hooks for hanging coats, umbrellas and hats, for example.

NOT IDEAL! There are loads of scattered objects with no order.
- Messy piles of magazines have stacked up over time.

- Dirty cups and other trash have begun to accumulate.
- Your living space is filled with things that don't add value to the function and aesthetics of the room.
- Moths and pets have attacked the blankets and throws.
- Toys for kids or dogs have erupted everywhere like a volcano.
- Loads of stuff cluttered around the entrance makes the whole room appear small and messy, even when it isn't.
- An abundance of personal items makes it hard for the buyers to see themselves living in this space.

SHOWTIME! Your living space shows buyers that it is a place of connection, warmth and energy. It cannot be too overbearing or oozing with your personality now that you are selling.

- Consider the concept of depersonalizing the space. Check whether it's appropriate to tone down colors that others may find outrageous, especially if it is something the realtors or estate agent mentioned when you brought them in for your first evaluations.
  Or is that beige just *too* beige and boring and the space could really do with a pop of bright, trendy color?
- If you have an excess of photos displayed, then perhaps you could pack some into the Ready-packed boxes. The same applies to too many ornaments or knick-knacks.
- If you have any storage facilities such as built-in closets, kists and drawers, then this would be the day to clear them out, especially if they are fixtures being sold with the property.
- Be mindful of what you are storing in these hidden areas – ideally, each drawer has one purpose only. This can add to the overall yet invisible 'feel' of the space. While most people won't open the drawers of stand-alone furniture because it is implied that it belongs to you and will be moving with you, you ought to be

prepared and willing for buyers to open all fixed closet or storage space.

- Check the quality of your cushions, throws, blankets, and lounge suite. Does anything need tossing, recycling or repairing? Sometimes just changing the cushions or even the covers and displaying new colorful candles can positively impact a room immediately and support the effortless sale of your home.
- If necessary, get a friend with a good design or decorating eye to help you depersonalize yet keep friendly, updated and inviting. Or you could enlist the support of professional home stagers to truly maximize the space and enhance all the right features of your home.

DAY 18

Did you skip gleefully into your lounge this morning knowing that you had cleared out some area yesterday, if not most of the space?

I hope you're reveling in the results of your hard work and appreciating all the shifts you have been making.

Divine dining room

There is less to read today, so let's just get to it! Everything relevant to the living space applies to today's task area, with the possible addition of looking at your seating arrangements and where you eat.

***IDEAL:* WELCOMING HAVEN** This space should always be ready to welcome guests. As you clear your dining-room space today, imagine that at any given time guests can arrive and you will be able to seat them at the table for a meal. If you have a sideboard or any other type of similar storage facility in the room, it should be reserved for accessories that contribute to the function of the room, and contain cutlery, table linen, napkins, serving dishes and perhaps candles. Try to keep all your passages and doorways clear of clutter to allow for maximum flow in and out of all rooms.

NOT IDEAL! The dining table tends to be the space where everything is dumped as you enter: laptops, groceries, school bags and pictures. Allocate a special place in the home for dumping, just *not* the dining table. If you are using your dining table as a desk, which is sometimes necessary, then ensure you have a system in place that means you are able to pack it all away quickly and easily and can eat around the table in five minutes flat.

SHOWTIME! Remember the concept of your home as a guesthouse and start seeing it through your *buyer's eyes* – you are now merely caretaking the space until the day you move out. The whole point of doing all this work is to become the ultimate buyer of your home in your mind. When someone walks into your home, the energy should lift, not slump. This also means that at any given time, your potential buyer could pop over unannounced and you will feel no stress.

DAY 19

Let's briefly recap some important things to bring them top of mind:

- Every time you clear out your physical clutter, you should ideally have six boxes or bags with you, so that you can easily delegate an item to one of the areas.

- While you are clearing your clutter, remember your initial intention, so that clutter clearing has a more significant purpose: *In order to sell my home with grace and ease, today I am letting go of all that no longer serves me.*

- Drink plenty of water every day to ease the letting-go process and to stay well hydrated. Clearing clutter and moving home can be exceptionally emotional and stressful and your body will be facing a physical and emotional toll. Right now, go grab some water.

As we kick off the last week, take some time to address the different boxes if you are doing it as we go along.

- **Rubbish:** You have hopefully been throwing out the trash generated from any given area immediately to signal the final end of that task.

- **Recycling:** Choose some items from this box, even if you can't do them all, and get those to wherever you wish to send them. You could call up charity shops and they will collect stuff from you. If any of the items belong to someone else, make the call today to arrange for them to collect their stuff. Action-ing just one thing will make you feel fabulous.

- **Repairs:** Take constructive action today – even if it means making a phone call to book an item in for repair, or to actually do it yourself, or plan when to do it.

- **Relocate:** If you haven't already naturally placed these items in their correct home this week, do so today. Walk around your home placing stuff where they rightfully belong. Remember the concept that pretty much everything you own has its own home. If the ideal place – where it needs to go – is not yet sorted and cleared, you can choose to leave it in the Relocate box for now.

- **Re-sell:** How are you going to sell these items – jumble sale, bid-or-buy, eBay, Gumtree, local shop for antiques and collectibles, auction or donate to household staff?

- **Ready-packed:** Seal and label all the Ready-packed boxes you have filled. Either label with the contents inside or – as I prefer – simply number the boxes, and keep a corresponding list with the contents of each box. Another idea is to take a picture on your phone of the open box to show the general contents because that will spark the memory of the whole box, and then store the image on your mobile device.

Storing ready-packed boxes Place all sealed boxes neatly in a storeroom, the garage or the spare bedroom in a way that doesn't hinder the buyer's ability to view the house. Some clients even choose to send boxes offsite for a short while to keep the home even more spacious and clear.

And now for today's specific task ... Note that your office is split into two sections over three days. Today we tackle your desk space and over the next two days your filing system.

Ditch your dodgy desk

I suspect that, as a result of the lessons you have been absorbing and executing over the past two weeks, there may have been some natural shifts in how you keep things. Any tidier? As you look at your desk today, notice whether there have been any subtle changes lately?

When it comes to the space you work at every day, be it in an office at work or a study at home, you need to think about your energy. Contemplate the meaning of your work, specific outcomes and productivity. Are you able to find things effortlessly when you need them and is your work 100% up to date? When your desk is free of clutter, looks professional and is inspiring, then it is that much easier to feel positively compelled to work, to work well, and to work productively. This is true for the home executive paying domestic bills as well as a top executive running a company! A messy, cluttered desk just keeps your head fuzzy and your logic stagnant.

IDEAL: A REFLECTION OF YOU Your desk reflects whom you are and how you wish to work. You can find things immediately, feel organized and in control of this space.

- Imagine leaving your desk 100% clear at the close of every single workday, so that when you see your desk first thing in the morning, your energy levels are elevated and you're keen and willing to get stuck in (just like you leave your bedroom the way you wish to come back to it every night).
- Having some form of notice board, pin board or whiteboard for reminders can be useful in keeping your work surface clear.

- Your desk has more free space than cluttered space. Think of the ideal ratio as 80% free space and 20% used space (remember the kitchen surfaces?) Mmmm, what is your current desk ratio?
- At most, your desk has the following:

    computer or laptop

    phone

    printer (this could also be next to your desk to allow for additional clear space)

    diary or desk calendar

    stationery holder

    personal items

    an in-tray system for processing current paperwork

- Depending on your personal needs, you may need different trays but at least consider having three or four:

    For Immediate Action

    To Pay

    To File

    To Read

- Open your mail regularly, toss out the envelopes and junk mail immediately, and then place each piece of correspondence in the appropriate tray, thus handling each just *once*. Everything else should be filed (we will get to this tomorrow) or stored.

Okay, now let's get cracking …

1. Clear your desk of *everything* right now. Everything.
2. Clean your desk, wiping with a damp cloth or a buff with furniture polish.
3. Decide what lifts your energy and is 100% necessary.
4. Make sure you have about 80% free space.
5. Create a simple system of trays for your current work.
6. When you leave your desk at night, remove all the clutter (including coffee cups and plates) and leave your desk ready to spring into action.
7. Empty your waste-paper bin every day.
8. Enjoy the feeling of knowing you will be greeted by a clear desk in the morning.
9. If you use a pinboard, remove unnecessary items so that it is clear and focused, not filled with loads of notes or Post-It stickers.

NOT IDEAL! Avoid a situation in which 80% of your desk is cluttered with food, cups, papers and loads of reminder notes so that there is no sense of order. Can anyone else come to your desk and make sense of it if you are out of the office and have an emergency work issue?

SHOWTIME! Place something beautiful on your desk: flowers, a plant, crystals or anything that evokes your work purpose and inspires you. An inspirational quote or saying on your desk is also great for creating a successful mindset. It's also good to have something personal, such as *one* family photo – remember the rule of not showing TOO much personal stuff.

Be 100 % prepared – create a 'Moving House' folder
As you are organizing your desk and papers, start thinking about all the services that you will need to cancel or inform of a change of address when you move home – insurance, gas, water, rates, tax office and

newspaper deliveries, for instance. If you come across these on your desk as you clear out, create a specific 'Moving House' folder for them. You want to have those documents on hand so it is easy to implement when the time comes and doesn't add further stress to the moving period.

DAY 20

After tackling your desk yesterday, I trust that there is a hint of excitement as the possibility of handling some dreaded paperwork and getting it sorted looms closer? While some people find paperwork impossible, others merely difficult and a few souls even easy and energizing, I have yet to come across anyone who *loves* doing their own paperwork. It is just one of those tasks that, on completion, will give you a feeling of relief and a sense of order, but very seldom elicits unmitigated joy ...

Fling your files (Part 1)

My angle when it comes to your filing is to focus on the benefit of having it all up to date. Knowing you will no longer lose even a minute's sleep worrying about where important documents are, or lose any vital energy stressing about the mess in your filing system, is a great goal to strive for. It's a treat to have a simple filing system that accommodates your life and work needs.

Another way of taking the process beyond the mundane is applying the rule of Legacy: 'If I were to die today, have I left my life in acceptable order for my loved ones to clear up after me?'

Remember, too, the tip from yesterday about keeping documents relevant to the 'moving house' in a specific folder. Do you really want to be lugging any old paperwork to your new home?

I know that it can seem so much easier to collect all the stuff in your life than it is to toss it out, so remember to keep your overall focus in mind: *I am selling with grace and ease.*

You can complete this – I know you can!
'Filing' is the one word that conjures up loads of anxiety in most people. So, whether it is home or office filing, it all amounts to the same thing: how structured and ordered you are in keeping everything in the right place.

If you loathe doing something, chances are it will create havoc in your life and waste hours of your time. For example, if you hate filing and can't be bothered to keep things in the right place and let everything pile up, then complete chaos ensues. Why?

You will spend hours looking for documents, which in turn reinforces how much you hate filing because you now have to wade through shoddy piles of papers – enough to make the hair on your head frizz and the 'overwhelmed' button to hit overdrive!

My aim is that, after completing this process once, you will never have to do it to these extremes again. It will become a way of life. You will never again have to commit this level of time and energy and will be able to keep on top of everything in your life in a healthier and more productive way.

FACT: The average US executive wastes six weeks per year searching for missing information in messy desks and files. (That translates into one hour per day.) – *The Wall Street Journal*, Esselte study

IDEAL: IT'S ALL ABOUT RETRIEVAL You should be able to retrieve any paperwork within 30 seconds.

- As soon as you hold any piece of paperwork in your paws you know exactly what to do with it immediately. You handle each document only once, by doing one of the following with it:

    You either *bin* or *shred* it immediately

    File it away in its proper 'home' for future reference and retrieval

    Delegate it to the relevant person to action

Place it in one of your current working piles for you to *action* (one of the in-trays created yesterday)

- Filing is weird in that it includes 'physical' pieces of paper, bills, forms and policies, for example, but – due to the nature of it – can also be considered 'energetic' clutter. So much of what the paper represents to us goes beyond what we see before us. So when your filing is up to date, not only will it physically affect your space more positively, but it will also make you feel more in tune with yourself, prouder, more organized, more up to date and thus more committed to excellence.

- Remember that when you are filing, you are doing so for one reason only: Easy retrieval!

- There are a few of ways to file all your paperwork, so you need to pick one that works for you. This should correspond with how you are naturally inclined to sort through things in your head when you think about them. What is the first way you would describe your car, for example? When you think about your car, do you think 'motor vehicle', 'transport' or 'Jeep'? And how would you file it for retrieval? The three most common filing methods are:

1. Alphabetically – A could include *Air-conditioner manual* and *AA membership*; B could include *Beth's school reports* and *Birth certificate*; C could include *Contracts* and *Car statements*; T could include *Tax* and *Telephone bills*.

2. According to broad categories specific to the different aspects or areas of your life,
   forexample: *Travel, Insurance, Cars, Guarantees, Mortgage, Banking , Kids*.

3. According to a color code: green for *Garden*, blue for *Home*, red for *Work*.

- Whichever filing method you choose, you may want to keep an index sheet that reminds you where everything is filed just until you get used to it all.

NOT IDEAL! Your filing is months or even years out of date and you have piles of accumulated documents that are all cluttered together, and you have no idea what is where. If you were to look for something it would take you ages to figure out where to start looking, let alone actually locatethe information you need. Remember, too, that having business and personal papers mixed up together creates havoc.

Filing step by step
The first layer of filing is to gather all like pieces together so that everything in one category is finally together – remember the mantra: *Like with like.* Follow these easy steps:

Step 1: Collect all the bits of paper from around the house, empty the closet or drawers where most documents are kept and work in an area with lots of floor space.

Step 2: Clean the closet or storage from which you retrieved most of the documents.

Step 3: Have a pen and paper at hand to list the categories.

Step 4: Pick up one document at a time and decide which category it would fall under by thinking about how you would retrieve it when you need it.

Step 5: Write the title of that category on scrap paper, and start a section on the floor for all other bits of paper that will fall under that category.

Step 6: Continue with each document, one by one.

Step 7: Throw trash and unnecessary paperwork out as you go.

Step 8: You will end up with several piles (or 'categories') that can now be filed appropriately.

Establishing a system: I am often asked, 'Where is the best place to store all my filing?' The choices are typically as follows:

- a simple concertina-type file bought at any stationary store if you do not have too much paperwork
- lever-arch files
- good old-fashioned steel filing cabinets with hanging files
- stacked stationary holders with drawers (bought ones typically have about six drawers)
- a 'tidy file' system with sturdy plastic holders and paper filing sleeves (available from any good-quality stationers)

Tips

- Generally, I do not recommend using cardboard boxes for your filing system. Boxes stacked with paper stored horizontally rather than vertically make it more difficult to retrieve documents because you have to wade through the entire contents to find something at the bottom of the pile! Boxes are great for archiving old paperwork though!
- Parkinson's Law tells us that: 'A task swells in perceived complexity and enormity in direct relation to the time allotted for its completion.' So just do it! Don't think that because we are dedicating two days to filing, you will leave it for tomorrow to get stuck in. You will need to allocate your full two hours anyway because this is usually a big task for everyone. Give yourself time by spreading it out over two days to get on top of it and make a big dent.

Move it!
As mentioned previously, keep adding documents to your "moving house' file i.e. all the relevant services that you will need to cancel or inform of a change of address plus any other paperwork you will require for the sale and transfer of the house – mortgage, deeds, lawyers' letters from your

purchase, contracts, release forms from police (and inland revenue if necessary) and any other relevant paperwork for the sale.

SHOWTIME! I highly recommend you also start a HOME-OWNER FILE for documents that can be passed on to the new buyer – information about maintenance of the home, paint colors, the sealant used for the built-in desk, the irrigation system, information about certain fixtures or warranties and guarantees that are still valid. Add in any proof of what maintenance work was done and when, including all the contractors who have worked on the property (plumbing, geysers, electrical and electric gates, for instance), as well as copies of guarantees or warranties relevant to them.

By creating this home-owner file, you can show it to buyers when they come to view. Imagine how impressed they will be when they realize how organized and how much care you take with your home? It will help assure them that you are reliable, trustworthy and responsible, thus making this a great buy with no buyer's remorse. This is going above and beyond and indicates the level of your commitment to *selling*!

DAY 21

Welcome to Day 2 of sorting out your filing system. Are you pulling your hair out or are you feeling fabulous? Maybe a bit of both? Paperwork requires persistence, so keep at it today.

Try the recommended addition of music or a friend to keep you on track.

Fling your files (Part 2)
Working with speed can help – decide within three seconds where the document needs to go. No dithering, just decisions.

Scrunching up the ones to toss out can add to your energy. Heck, you can even try to have fun while doing it – remember what it is that you wish to manifest. You can take the expanding pile of trash and recycle it, or it might be more appropriate for you to burn it if some documents are highly confidential or carry an emotional "charge" for you; find a way to transmute them.

Getting rid of old documents and ordering the ones you are storing is a powerful sign to the universe that you are creating good space for more opportunities and adventures to come your way because you will have freed up time and energy to do other things now.

Tip

- Filing can be an area that causes unspeakable stress and anxiety. If so, it may be useful to call in someone to help – an organized friend, colleague or an organizing professional such as myself to get 100% on top of this. (Check in your country for the relevant professional association of organizers – www.napo.net in the USA.)

DAY 22

Before we proceed with today's task, check in honestly about how you are doing with all the maintenance, cleaning and sprucing actions you scheduled after you completed your initial assessment. Are you on track with your time frames or do you need to pay more deliberate attention to get it all complete?

It is also time to re-look at your first Reveal date. On Day 5 it was suggested to set your show day or ready-to-take-appointments date so that you have a specific time frame to work toward.

Call the realtors/estate agents back so that they can see your new-look home, and make a decision as to your way forward – are you going to work with several realtors/agents simultaneously, sign a sole mandate or sell privately? You will be finishing off the big areas over the following few days (think garage, storerooms and loft, for instance) so you will be ready in a very short space of time. If you didn't do so at Step 5, then it is time to schedule your first show day and let the world know you are coming out to play and that you mean business! If you have been getting everything ready to the point where a home stager or decorator will come in for final professional touches, it might be time to call on them now.

Acknowledge your progress
The following is a list to remind you of all the amazing preparation work you have been doing; it should boost your energy so that you can give today and tomorrow the last blast for good measure. We have covered the following in daily order:

- Bedroom (including your bedside table and under your bed)
- Bathroom (including your cabinets and storage)
- Closet (including shoes, and clothing both shelved and hanging)
- Kitchen (including cabinets, refrigerator and freezer)
- Crockery, cutlery and appliances
- Books and magazines
- Music
- Living space
- Dining room
- Desk
- Filing

Your choice of indoors section
And here we are today! Isn't it great to look back and see what shifts you have made as you embark on your move? As you plan for today, remember the basics of your six boxes, and how to go about clearing an area from start to finish – I bet it is forever etched in your psyche. Most importantly, whenever you are letting go of something that no longer serves you, remember to work with your mindful intention so that you make space for something more meaningful to show up in your life: *In*

order to sell my home with grace and ease, today I am letting go of that which no longer serves me.

I would like you to spend time today in one of the other areas that have probably been gathering clutter for ages. But I'm going to give you a few options because we all live in different spaces and in different-sized homes so one may be more appropriate for you than another. Remember that at the end of the book, you may need to redo or complete several areas if you had oodles of clutter to start with. Pick one of the following areas to concentrate on today:

- **Kids' rooms:** If you have children and they have not yet cottoned on and cleared out their rooms (or if they are too young), get cracking in one of those.
- **Spare room:** If you have an extra room that has been driving you nuts, go for this space!
- **Linen closet:** You could focus on your linen and towels that need clearing – as well as everything else that may have found its way into the linen closet. This is one of those areas that buyers love to see super organized and there is a weird correlation between how your linen closet is organized and how buyers perceive you and your home. In other words, *it matters* that your linen closet isn't in tatters.
- **Trunks and kists:** These inevitably start to overflow as the members of the household consider it an all-purpose storage facility for the day-to-day use of everyone in the home. They're not. They need to serve a purpose.
- **TV/playroom/den:** If you don't already have one, then it's probably on your wish list. But these multipurpose rooms are generally the first to succumb to the Dumping Ground Syndrome. Because we have been concentrating our attention on the better-used living spaces in your home, these last few areas can be quite a big task to tackle.

Tip

- Remember to keep the primary function of the room top of mind and do not confuse the spaces. This helps the buyer to know immediately what to do with the space. So pick an area you can zap today!

Kids' rooms

Usually, from the age of three upwards, kids can start being co-responsible for their space. Teach them to respect their space from a young age, and lay some ground rules for tidying up, whether once a week or every day. Every time you do it *for* them, you're failing them by not teaching them rules, boundaries or how to look after and respect their belongings.

Teach your children the 'One in, one out' rule with toys, and use particular times of the year to clear out – holidays, birthdays and religious holidays – to make space for new or age-appropriate toys.

If you have or are planning to have more children, you may well fall into the fairly common trap of wanting to keep it all for the younger child. When clothes or toys are no longer appropriate for the older child, box them up, mark the carton properly and remove them to another storage area (such as the spare room or the garage).

The spare room/guest room

Ideally, the guest room should always be ready to receive guests; these rooms should have hanging and shelf space for guests' belongings; the bedside tables are completely empty; and the closet space is neatly packed. You want guests to feel welcome and not that they've been relegated to the junk room. The aim is a homely bed-and-breakfast feeling!

Linen closet

As a rule, each bed in your home ideally needs three sets of linen: one on the bed, one in the wash cycle and one for spare just in case. You can either store your entire home's linen in one common space –think a passage or hall closet, for example – or you can keep each room's linen in that room. Choose whichever option makes sense to you and your space. Buyers definitely look inside linen closets – it's one of those weird anomalies that they will positively resonate with and smile at one packed with hotel-like precision.

If you choose to keep all your linen in one place, you need to decide how you would like to store it for easy retrieval:

- Like with like: all pillowcases together, double sheets together, duvet covers in different sizes, for example – and then label the shelves so that everyone knows what belongs where
- Room by room: each room's linen together in one place, labeled with the owner's name
- Set by set: one whole set together for each bed, complete with sheets, pillowcases and duvet covers in one pile, with spares in their own piles.

The TV/playroom/den
These rooms are usually common-space areas and require vigilance so that everyone knows the rules of the place. Make sure that you have enough storage to make the space easy on the eye, and to make tidying up a cinch. Install extra shelves, and CD or DVD racks as needed. Use bookshelves and magazine holders to contain objects in their rightful space. Kists and trunks are great for toys. Keep remotes, cables and plugs neatly stored so that the space is safe and user-friendly. If your pets are staying on site for show days or appointments, make sure that pet areas are neat and hygienic.

Move it!
Get creative with pre-packing up toys, hobbies, crafts and excess of anything that you are choosing to keep but don't use often – keep getting a head start on your packing and simultaneously create the illusion of lots of space.

Don't forget the outbuildings
Do not underestimate the effect of the outbuildings on your property on the sale of your home. You will have to move it all anyway, so the next few days are allocated to these areas to be truly complete. Take another look at your assessment from the first week, to bring what needs to be done top of mind.

The following areas are often where we have hidden many layers and collective years of clutter, because we don't always have to look at these spaces that much and have simply been able to ignore them for long periods:

- Garden shed
- Workshed
- Garage
- Basement
- Storeroom
- Attic

Move it!
I suggest you get some help from friends and family or hire laborers for the next few days, or get in a professional organizer to speed things up because areas such as outbuildings can be a real challenge. You may even want to postpone these last tasks to the weekend when you can dedicate a little more time and muscle power. If these larger areas out of control, then call in some expert assistance. Take a look at my website to read about what people experience when I come bouncing through their doors www.kate-emmerson.com and support them.

Remember that your home is not ready for sale until every last part of your home, its outbuildings and garden are complete!

Have a fabulous, energized chucking-out day!

DAY 23

We've accomplished much over the last few weeks, and yesterday's task was probably one of the most difficult and time-consuming. But we're nearly there, so let's give it one last shot to get the big spaces done and dusted.

The final push!

Most of the big spaces harbor the really old, old stuff that has been lurking there forever, so you need to harness your superpowers of tenacity and determination and do what needs to be done. Stay as focused as possible, using the energy created from the past clearing to support these bigger areas.

Keep only what you need and will use – and be extra strict in these big areas as we tend to have more space to keep stuff 'just in case!' Storerooms, attics, basements and garages typically have old items bought but never used, piles of wood for one day never, and lots of larger items to throw out, so remember to call in additional muscle power to help.

Focus on the end result, knowing that you have completed every last nook and cranny. Apply everything you have learned and implemented to zap this area *fast*. Use every ounce of insight, knowledge and skill and apply it in super clutter-clearing form.

PART 4
SHOWTIME: Selling with grace and ease

Finally, the time has come to reap the rewards of all your hard work. Your upcoming sale and move day will undoubtedly be vastly different to any other you have experienced in your lifetime. You have done the work, so *trust* that now. Relax into the process. Working your way through Part 1, you released attachment from this space and embedded the awesome memories to take with you. No one can take that away from you now. All those processes will allow the final goodbye and all the necessary administrative tasks roll out more elegantly and won't stress you out as much.

Allow yourself to simply enjoy the space now, thinking of your home as a house – perhaps even a holiday space to enjoy, no longer attached to it as your home. Spend time envisioning your next step and accepting what is about to unfold for you and your family. Dare to allow it to be effortless and actually welcome it.

Selling this property is now about switching gears and becoming buyer-centric. Think about engaging the buyers' senses and, most importantly, the emotions of the buyers from the moment they enter your property. From this moment forward it's all about *The Buyer*, not you! You have your ultimate sale price you will accept in mind; now keep yourself out of the way and allow it to happen with speed, ease and grace.

This last section is designed to help you stay crystal clear about this phase. I share with you how to stay in show day mode, ruthless yet clear and thus welcoming this sale with speed. It's also vital for you to choose the very best way to sell this property. Are you doing it privately or via estate agents or realtors, or as a sole mandate? Give yourself the best chance to get the property on the market and sold in record time. It's going to be super fast because you have paved the way, so expect serendipitous events to unfold.

Wrapping it up

Here are some final thoughts to consider before showtime – your show day or viewing by appointment.

- **Boxes:** Ensure that you timeously and appropriately *process* the contents of all the boxes you have filled during the clutter-clearing tasks.
- **Rubbish:** Get all the trash offsite as soon as possible. Call someone to collect and dispose of, if need be.
- **Recycling:** Arrange for charity shops to collect, distribute to friends or drop off at a recycling depot. Return items to rightful owners with 24 hours.
- **Repairs:** What *still* needs to be fixed? Schedule it now to empty this box.
- **Relocate:** Move the contents of this box to the appropriate spot or room.
- **Re-sell:** Make time this week to get the remaining items in this box out of your space and get the cash in hand!
- **Ready-packed:** Make sure that all these boxes are appropriately sealed and labeled to make move day a cinch. They all need to be neatly packed in a specific space, such as the garage, or in temporary storage offsite until you relocate.

The final countdown

- Deal breakers: Double check with your neighbors or your realtor/estate agent if there are any current 'deal breakers' you should be aware of when answering buyers' questions. Think about schools, new shopping centers, housing developments, or any new laws being passed, for instance.
- If you haven't already, you need to commit a date for your show day and when you will start accepting appointments to view this house.

- Re-evaluate your property assessment to double check that everything on your initial list to spruce up or repair has now been now ticked off.
- Re-check that all the entrances to the property are spotless to enhance that initial first impression and curb appeal.
- Double check that your house smells fresh. Invest in good-quality air or linen spray. No fake coffee – vanilla please!
- Beds should always be beautifully made – think guesthouse mode.
- Make sure the bathrooms and toilets are spotless and smell fresh.
- Closets and cupboards need to be impeccably tidy *inside*.
- Alert the neighbors so that they are mindful of noise for the next few hours – you don't want a once-off crazy party next-door scaring off potential buyers.
- Curtains and blinds should be opened at the right angle for maximum light.
- Cut back any bushes close to windows, thus allowing more light to stream in. *Light sells properties!*
- Turn on appropriate lights to highlight certain features.
- Play unobtrusive music; choose appropriately, depending on your target market.
- Consider setting the dining table (home stagers tip!).
- Help viewers understand the main *function* of each space; for example, place a beautifully laid tea tray with a cup saucer, spoon, teapot, sugar and even a book open at your favorite reading spot overlooking the garden.
- Do not assume that buyers will instantly be able to interpret a space. Make it as obvious as possible for them to see themselves living here.

At the last minute ...

- Clear up last-minute pet and kid mishaps
- Tidy all toys away
- Ensure that the pool is sparkling blue, no matter what the season
- Turn on the water feature to create a tranquil atmosphere
- Turn the garden sprinklers off – potential buyers may want to walk though the garden.
- Consider taking your pets' offsite for showday! Some buyers are terrified of dogs, allergic to cats or phobic about birds and it will put them off immediately. Often buyers will not even enter the space if they feel uncomfortable – what a shame.

The game changers

Certain game changers are sure to sweeten the deal to ensure selling with ease and speed!

Photographs
Consider showcasing beautiful images of your property as a scrolling slideshow on your computer. Show different times of the day, year, season, mood, unusual angles – a very effective, upmarket touch to show off the house in all its glory. Of course, if you are using a realtor/estate agent, there will be professional photographs or videos on their website, but these can be *your* favorite ones taken over the years. My brother, Jem, introduced me to a very cool concept over and above this showcasing of photographs: if you have done any major renovations to the property, show those pictures of transformation, offering some sense of history of how the current property came to be in its current state of glory. People are fascinated by 'before' and 'after' photos. This will help them feel emotionally involved with the space.

Remember, though, to keep these photos fairly neutral and depersonalized so that they show off the house and the property, rather than all the people or animals living there. Having said that, one or two pics of big events or special occasions when everything was beautifully laid out could add a lovely touch and show buyers what is possible in the entertainment areas.

Home-owners file
Make sure that the home-owners file you created is visible and available to page through. The one you created with everything house related for effortless continuity: security, staff, history (house plans, for instance), warranties, guarantees, manuals for the irrigation and sound systems, renovations done and paint swatches, for example.

When potential buyers know that you have everything on tap to pass onto them, they will be in awe of how you have looked after this space they want to call home. Make it *easy* for them.

Showtime mindset
To reiterate - you are now the designated caretaker of this beautiful space, holding the fort until the rightful new owner comes along. From now on, it is a *house* ready to be sold, more than a *home* that you live in. It feels warm, beautiful and inviting but is not overcrowded with your personality and stuff. Potential buyers can easily envisage themselves living here and making it *their* home.

You have released all attachment to the house and are focused on a positive outcome: selling at the right price with speed and ease.

Trust that the work is done! Read your intention from Step 8 every day to stay in the right frame of mind and pave the way for the buyer to effortlessly find you.

Tip
- Remember to keep your home and state of mind in show-day condition until you get that offer to purchase *signed and the deal sealed*!

Time to sell
It is now time to get cracking with selling this beautiful, cleared and energized space by finally showcasing your property.

- I suggested you book an appointment with realtors/ estate agents at the very beginning, so be sure to activate this and get your home on the market now. Then make the decision whether you are selling it privately or through a realtor/agent and possibly a sole mandate to get additional support, commitment and service. Some realtors/agents will also have access to, or even include, the services of home stagers to showcase your property at the maximum level. Remember that we are aiming for minimal days on the market because the longer your home is listed as For Sale, the less the house is perceived as desirable, or buyers will tend to offer much lower prices. Whichever option you choose, get professional pictures and even videos taken and confirm the date for your show day/appointments.

- Allocate small, ongoing chores for *everyone* (over the age of five, at least) who lives under the roof – regardless of age, everyone can help.

- Get everyone on the same page about selling your home and why it's important to keep it viewer ready.

- Remember that the house is now on show – and, energetically, that means all the time. Your ideal buyer could drive past and fall in love with the outside and want to pop in *now*.

- Be prepared to sell fast! Believe me, it *will* happen sooner than you ever dreamed possible – that is the power of getting clear in both your heart and home.

- Keep your home organized and clutter free so that it will never take you more than 20 minutes in total to get ready for viewing.

- Place fresh flowers in strategic places, and change them regularly.

- Always have room fresheners handy for that last-minute spritz. Splurge on good-quality room fragrance.

- Enjoy the lightness in your step knowing that, on a practical level, *this* move will be the easiest one of your life because you have already clutter-cleared, organized and pre-packed up some boxes.
- Stay positive: *The perfect buyer is falling in love with this home and freeing me up for the next step. I am ready to let go and move on!*
- Trust yourself and your realtor/estate agent to do the job properly.
- Think *guesthouse*, think *buyer*, think *Sold* from now on.
- Where relevant, alert your household staff and give them the appropriate information timeously.

Keep it clear
Here are a few practical tips to keep your space clear and clutter free in the run-up to show day.

Daily: It takes just a few minutes to make sure everything is in top form.
- Keep your bedside table tidy at all times.
- Leave your bedroom immaculate, as though your home is a guesthouse.
- Throw household trash into outside bins and clean those bins often.
- Always wash the dishes and wipe the sink until it shines.
- Leave your desk clear at the close of every day.
- Stick to the rule: *Put things back in their proper 'home'.*
- To reduce what needs to be moved, use up what is already in the cupboards, refrigerator and freezer.

Weekly: The following are some practical suggestions on how to keep your space ready for viewing:
- Always make sure the main property entrance is clear, clean and welcoming. *Always.* That first impression governs how the

buyer *feels* and it takes extra effort to turn around a negative first impression.

- Ensure your clothing is put away neatly - remember they open closets.
- Keep all living spaces clear...do an extra half-hour blitz weekly.
- Relocate anything that has gone astray back to its proper *home*.
- Action your in / out tray on your desk to keep the *flow* of energy.
- Clear the 'hot-spot' you created usually in kitchen/ entrance
- Attend immediately to last-minute marks, spills, scuffs or repairs on carpets, tiles, floorboards or furniture.
- Ensure that the entire space is kept clean, organized and welcoming.

Easy transfer

Keep all your relevant and necessary paperwork you have gathered together in your 'moving house' folder in a handy spot, ready for the transfer of the property once the sale is activated: mortgage or bond, deeds, lawyers' letters from your purchase, contracts, release forms from police and inland revenue, property tax and any other relevant paperwork for the sale.

Your final goodbye

Consider having a ritual evening to say your final goodbye. If it resonates with you and is your kind of 'thing,' light some candles or incense, make a special dinner and do a final 'close-out.' Read through some of the work you did in Part 1 to emotionally detach yourself and perhaps build that bonfire to burn what you wrote – especially all the challenges you faced here. You could also walk through the entire space, room by room, saying one final goodbye and emotionally *intending* to take all the good with you, while leaving all the challenges behind.

Share your stories
I would LOVE to hear about how this process shifted this house sale for you! Plus, others embarking on the same process will benefit from hearing your stories of success and just how quickly you shifted the sale of your property by following this process. Please share your thoughts and ideas on my Facebook group - come and brag about what happened to you over here: www.facebook.com/groups/352379831623938

Proof and praise for SHIFT YOUR HOME

Life changing stories from real people selling their homes!

Natalie and Vincent *After just two show houses we sold our house and we were happy with the very FIRST offer we received!*

Sean *I am still quite in awe that within just two days of doing the processes with you I received my very first offer.*

Lesley *I received two cash offers, both higher than my asking price, within one day of putting it on the market and the sale was finalized within a week.*

Cheryl Reum (Keller Williams Premier Estate Agent) *This is a home seller's bible! I would heartily recommend this publication to every estate agent out there as a gift on a mandate granted to help sellers. Endorsed unreservedly.*

Lynne and Petie *Our home was on the market with three different agents over 13 months, yet within just 11 days of doing Kate's work, I accepted an Offer to Purchase! We finished the exercises on 5 June 2016 and received the written offer on 16 June 2016.*

Marilu and Ryan *It came down to two buyers that were 'betting' for our home. We recommend anyone looking for the most seamless, stressless sale of their home to make use of Kate's program.*

Hannetjie *Our home had been on the market for a year and we are so grateful that the sale was confirmed a little more than a month after my first contact with Kate and her program.*

Fiona *Even two weeks before our designated show day we had effortlessly signed the sale of agreement!*

Rieks *The most profound book ever when you are selling or moving house!*

Pauline *It's really important to do the emotional disconnection letter, if I hadn't then I would still be floundering and running around in ever increasing circles.*

Brigitte *The energy of the house already feels lighter and the rooms feel more spacious and make it easier for me to let it go – with love.*

Debi *I definitely feel in me a complete shift of energy and lightness ...*

Radia *Thank you for opening my eyes – I re-sold my house to ME! There's no denying it, Kate, your system works!*

Tracey *I don't believe I could have done this without your help Kate, the exercises really made an enormous difference to the way I looked at things. Holding onto something because you believe its security is not always the right thing to do.*

MORE STORIES TO INSPIRE YOUR JOURNEY:
These are the unique stories of clients who followed this process when selling their home, just like you are!

Natalie says: *After just two show houses we sold our house!* I was smart enough to get a copy of Kate's book to help us *shift our home*. We were happy with the very *first* offer we received and after just two show houses we sold our house! Our estate agent said, 'Everybody loves your house.' I had had prior experience of Kate's de-cluttering work in our cottage, storeroom, office and closets. I definitely think the benefits of that initial work were long-lasting.

What really had an impact for me in regarding this book was:

- Further clutter clearing *before* selling makes packing so much easier.
- The importance of depersonalizing a house *before* you sell it.
- Saying goodbye to the house, with gratitude, *before* selling.

- Leaving very little evidence of the owners on showday.
- Kate's philosophy of packing like with like made it easy to prepare.
- My husband was thrilled with the results and asked if we could 'live like this all the time'!
- I was delighted to be able to redistribute goods of value that I am choosing not to take to our new home.

Life is about results; Kate's book works. It is also an energizing and hugely rewarding process.

Thank you, Kate! *Natalie Uren*

Shaun says: *I am still quite in awe that within just two days of doing the processes with you I received the first offer.* I really wanted to thank you for all your effort with helping me quickly and effectively shifting my property in a very short space of time. I am still quite in awe that literally two days after our first meeting, I received the first offer on the house and not much longer after that – and after doing some of your 'shifting' exercises – I concluded the big rental agreement.

I am a big believer in your kind of work and would highly recommend it to anybody stuck in a similar situation trying to sell or let their property. Your positivity, light, love and manner in which you make the 'shift' are superlative!
Thank you for your help!

Shaun Marais

Lesley says: *I received two cash offers, both higher than my asking price, within one day of putting it on the market and the sale was finalized within a week.* My daughter, Kate, (yes, this same author) surprised me with a visit to the UK to declutter me and my home as I was thinking of moving into a much smaller place. I had no idea how much stuff I had or what a hard job it would be.

We laughed, we drank lots of wine, we managed not to fall out and the weeks went by in a flash, but we got it done.

One week after she left, I put my Yorkshire bungalow on the market and had *two cash offers* within *one* day and it was sold in a week for a higher price than advertized. I have now bought an apartment in a retirement village. Moving will be so much easier now that all the clutter has gone.

Go on, folks, try it and see what happens for you.

Lesley Emmerson (Yes, Lesley's my mum, but I am a hard taskmaster when I believe in something and the proof was in the pudding! What she says here is absolutely true – especially about drinking all that wine! But, seriously, she did indeed sell her house this fast at a higher-than-original-asking price!)

Cheryl Reum (Keller Williams Premier Estate Agent) says: *This is a home seller's bible!*I am a real-estate agent of 30 years' standing and yet still fall under the same thinking as any other seller. I would heartily recommend this publication to every realtor/estate agent out there as a gift on a mandate granted to help Sellers. Endorsed unreservedly.

I had a real Ugly Duckling property to sell and was gearing up for an intense situation, when I just relaxed and implemented the wisdom shared by Kate. I have consolidated my life in the past 8 months and experienced all the angst of selling and stress and gut binding anxiety of previous sales. After absorbing this book into my pores - flow happened. I received an offer 7 days after the previous one collapsed - with immediate occupation, delightful purchasers who loved the potential, ignored the "no curb appeal" and proceeded to transfer within 6 glorious, stress-free weeks. Also, a piece of land that had sat forever unsold, an unclaimed Cinderella that did not even attract a hobnailed boot, sold to another agent at 25,000 more than my previous advertised desperate price. Today I received a closing offer on my last property in White River bringing an era to closure.

I have also shifted 4kg in the past month, baggage jettison deluxe. Until you move both your body, heart and mind out of a property, tenure will be guaranteed and sale difficult. Let it go and bring the winds of change as wisps of new joy into your life. All of the manifestation I am certain was as a result of the exercises done via Kate's advice. Magic or coincidence? You decide.

Cheryl Reum (Keller Williams Premier)

Lynne says: *Our home was on the market with three different agents over 13 months, yet within just 11 days of doing Kate's work, I accepted an Offer to Purchase! We finished the exercises on 5 June 2016 and received the written offer on 16 June 2016.*
My name is Lynne Scholtz. I am a 55-year-old mother of a 14-year-old son, Peter. When I decided to separate from my husband I thought it best to find a home near his, as we have a young child and wanted easy access for all parties involved.

I came across 1 Kings Place, which was previously used as a pre-school. (In fact, my son Peter had gone to the school for about three years as it was close to our home.) It had had a few owners since then and had been left to deteriorate, and no one was living in the house at the time.

The garden consisted of overgrown trees, sand instead of grass and a dirty, green, cracked pool. The house had cracks and was full of old furniture. Bathrooms and kitchen were in very poor condition.

I was able to see the value in the property but it would not be attained without a lot of hard work and money.

On 1 July 2013 the house was registered in my name; it was around this time that my father's health began to deteriorate, so the decision was made that he too would move into our new home with Peter and me. He had an unknown lung dystrophy, but if stationery could work as he always had.

My dad never had idle hands and even now, in his state of health, took on the challenge to redo the garden, build railings and burglar bars, fix and mend whatever he could; he worked tirelessly. He managed all the contractors and deliveries of goods to the house. In my eulogy for him after he passed away, I said that the garden would forever remind me of my dear father!

The house was also a new start for Peter and me, and we had so many happy times in this home. Albeit separated from his dad, he still got to see him every weekday going to school. The three years we lived there were some of the best in my life, and I would never have wanted to sell the property other than the fact that Peter decided he wanted to go to Michaelhouse for high school. Michaelhouse is a fulltime boarding school in the KZN Midlands. However, they are allocated Friday-night dinner passes, as well as some Saturday and Sunday day passes. It would be very difficult to commute from Johannesburg to the Natal Midlands for just a dinner pass or day pass, so I decided to give up everything and move closer to Peter's new school.

The moment I heard he had been accepted into Michaelhouse – 20 May 2015, my father's birthday – I contacted a friend who is a real-estate agent. She got busy right away. Although Parkhurst is a rather sought-after suburb, there was very little interest, and the one written offer fell apart with regards the bank granting the full bond.

In March 2016, I decided to get another real-estate agency involved, and once again very little interest. At the end of May, I got an offer *well below* the asking price and as it had taken so long and I wanted to move to KZN to be close to Peter I nearly accepted it. Thank goodness I did not. I met up with Kate and got a copy of her book.

I decided to get a third estate agent on board, together with the previous two. Then my son and I sat down and worked through Kate's book. We both wrote down our points and then read them to each other and discussed them. What the house meant to us and the memories we had to release. The good, the bad, the happy and the sad. We laughed, we shed tears, and through this process, I learned a lot more about my son and the things he values. I am sure he too learned a lot about me. The process was cathartic for both of us and it set in motion the sale of our home.

I would say that Step 1 was our best, as it was all about the positive stuff and let us reflect on so much that we can be thankful and grateful for in our lives.

We finished the exercises on 5 June 2016 and we received the written offer on 16 June 2016. It was slightly lower than the asking price, but I was more than happy with the offer, which I duly accepted.

The only additional stipulation that the buyer had in the offer to purchase was a request that we leave the hanging flower pots (that my dad put up) as part of the sale. This sent me the message that they will love the garden that my father created and gave me that added confirmation that *all was all right!*

Before working through *Shift Your Home*, I did not realize how strong the attachment is to a physical entity. But I have released this home and all the love that created it and moved on to create new exciting memories.

Lynne Scholtz

Marilu says: *It came down to two buyers that were 'betting' for our home. We recommend anyone looking for the most seamless, stress-less sale of their home to make use of Kate's program.* Before we met Kate, nothing shifted or happened in our approach to sell our city home ... Kate's exercises helped us to work through everything, accept the situations and understand what and why I was going through so much. Finally, we arrived at a place where we were both very comfortable in letting go. Now we are able to pay off our debt on the new home and have the life and home that we have always dreamed of.

This was definitely because of the hard work we had put in working with Kate. We are truly grateful for her input and guidance ...

I don't believe that anything happens by chance and felt that the day I saw Kate's post about helping people sell their homes, it was meant to be as we were in the process of selling. Well, we had already tried a few things to sell the house. From directly selling it on Facebook to getting agents to sell it for us. Nothing happened.

My husband and I have been the controversial couple that does things the 'other' way around. Part of this journey was a two-year stay in the middle of Johannesburg CBD – seen to be the most dangerous place to be – but we bought into the vision of reclaiming the inner city and uplifting the community. The idea was to live there for two years and then move on. (As that is what our gypsy life is like.) Our two-year mark was creeping closer, and with having our little girl in the process, it was time to move on. In mid-winter, hubby found us a beautiful new abode in the countryside and it was clear that the time had arrived for us to say goodbye to city living.

We have a life of no debt and we wanted to keep it this way going forward. In order to buy the new place and stay debt free, we decided to sell our property in mid-Johannesburg. Everything started to move really quickly, except the sale of our city apartment. It was at this point that Kate came into our lives and guided us through a very interesting reflective journey to complete our time in the city and embrace our new beginning. This journey entailed us having to do lots of homework, something that was initially not taken seriously as I fell short of time with baby and hubby coming home late every evening. Obviously nothing shifted or happened in our approach to sell our city home. Things started to press really hard, and finally we decided to finally give Kate's approach a real chance and we started with our homework.

I didn't think that I would be so attached to our place in the city, but as we were going through the reflective homework, I started to realize the intense emotional connection I had to this place, as well as the strange fears I had about moving on … Finally we arrived at a place where we were both very comfortable in letting go …

Now we are able to pay off our debt on the new home and have the life and home that we have always dreamed of.

This was definitely because of the hard work we had put in working with Kate. *Marilu Meiring*

Hannetjie says: *Our home had been on the market for a year and we are so grateful that the sale was confirmed a little more than a month after my first contact with Kate and her program.*
Our home had been on the market for one year when I received a call from Kate. She explained her process of de-cluttering – which I had already completed by that stage, so she then proceeded to send me a list of exercises to complete to assist with the process of emotional detachment and closure.

My husband and I spent one Friday evening reminiscing about the years we had spent in our home – which we planned and built – with great enjoyment about the good times but also some sad reflection regarding the sad times.

We are truly grateful for the time we were allowed to live in this beautiful home overlooking a dam in a small and quiet estate in Johannesburg.

I must also include the fact that prayer formed a fundamental part of our process, but we are grateful that the sale of our home was confirmed a little more than a month after my first contact with Kate. We are scaling down, which made the whole process more difficult.

I trust that you will have a similar experience when following Kate's guidelines.

Hannetjie Pretorius

Pauline says: *Kate's book has helped me enormously with the process of getting my house B & B Ready* (I love that expression as it says it all), to be able to put it on the market. I am relocating to another country which prompted me to do this process, I knew I couldn't get it done on my own and had read Kate's previous book. The instruction/advice was really easy to follow and often very amusing which appealed to me as it never felt as though there was any pressure being put on me – though she does kick ass sometimes. It's really important to do the emotional disconnection letter, if I hadn't then I would still be floundering and running around in ever increasing circles. Once I started clearing out I was able to release and resolve a lot of emotional baggage from the abusive relationship I had been in; the process also helped me find the courage to leave that relationship just by the sheer process of letting go and clearing out. The order in which one starts looking at the property is terrific as there are so many things we just don't see any longer. As to clearing out drawers and cupboards – wow how much we hold on to on a material as well as emotional level. That did take me a bit longer than I wanted but I realized that I had to be ruthless as none of those things brought me anything but dust and crammed drawers and cupboards. We don't need the material things to keep the memories, that's what our mind is for. Once you start getting rid of the smallest item your home seems to expand.

My lightbulb moment was when I turfed my bread bin! Just getting it out of the way seemed to just bring all this light and airiness into my kitchen. Such as simple act that can bring so much relief. I then lost 7kg's in the process of letting go of emotional baggage – I wasn't even trying or dieting!! Kate is always generous with advise and help so no need to feel alone.

I would highly recommend Kate's book on a multitude of levels. Pauline - South Africa

Rieks Swart says: *The most profound book ever when you are selling or moving house!* Can definitely recommend it to anyone who wants to gain better insight and understanding of all that is really happening around you during this transition we all have to go through at some point. This book really helped me to make the transition with ease. Thank you Kate!

Fiona says: *Even two weeks before our designated show day we had effortlessly signed the sale of agreement!* I have known Kate for about three years now and have worked through both her books *Clear Your Clutter* and *Ditch your Glitch*, and was also a member of her Dream to Draft Write Your Book Group this year. Everything that I have done with Kate has had a positive impact on my life. After a phone chat with Kate one evening when I told her that we were selling our house to follow a dream of owning a boat that we have been working towards for three years, Kate suggested we read *Shift Your Home*.

I printed the copy out and gave it to Jan and asked him to have a read through and see what he thought. The very next day I got a Whatsapp message from Jan:

'05/05. We should do what Kate suggested. She is ruthless. Her program in this book you gave me last night is not huge. It's quick and relentless. Clean up. Do you love it? Is It Useful? Does it add value and energy to my life? She says a lot about a little, but it means a lot to the emotional mind.'

We made the decision to prepare the house for showday and remove ourselves 'emotionally' from the house. We were relentless. We had three categories: what we need to take with us to our new life on a catamaran, what is sentimental to go into storage and what we are getting rid of.

The agents came to see us. We told them that we needed time to fix up a few things in and around the house and that we also had a holiday planned for July so it was decided that we would do our first show house the second weekend of August.

Emotional attachment: I needed to do all the exercises Kate offers of emotionally detaching myself from 'My Home'. I decided that I would spend time in each space of 'My Home' and allow the memories to come to me, pack up everything that was not needed in the room anymore and place it in one of the three categories that we had, and then to say goodbye and move on to the next space, leaving my favorite spot for last. I have learned with all of the courses that I have done with Kate that to take a comforting drink with you while doing a hard task is always a good idea, so armed with my big mug of coffee I headed for the loft, thinking to myself that this would be the easiest place to start. *Whoa!* Was I in for a shock!

Again Kate was right as every day, every hour and every minute that you spend in your home you build more and more emotional connections and memories. I found myself sitting on the floor of the loft in tears as all the memories of everything that had happened in this one space came flooding back ... Time became a blur for me as I remembered all that had happened in the eight years that I have lived in this house; I saw the excitement on the faces of the girls when they first found out that the loft was going to be their playroom, I remembered choosing the colors for the room and decorating it. Even though it was sad and tears streamed down my face, I also felt peace coming over me as the memories made me realize we had had such a good life here and that I will never forget the good. It took me a full five days to go through the house and say goodbye, store all the memories in my mind and walk away happy and thankful for everything.

The hardest part was our bedroom. This room had been my haven since the day we moved in and I had decorated it with love and passion, the same love and passion that Jan and I have.

Surely this is not possible ... Two weeks before that due date the agent phoned us and asked if they could bring through a couple to look at the house. At first, we were reluctant, but the agent assured us that the couple was aware the house was still not 'show-day ready'. That Sunday the couple came to view the house, while the agents were showing them through the house another couple arrived un-announced and asked if they could look at the house as well. That night we had a signed sale of agreement!

Afterward, the agent told us that when the buyers had walked through the house they could hear the woman saying to her husband, 'Hmmm ... we can put that painting there and there is space for this here and this can be the baby room – see how airy and light it is.' She also commented on the fact that she knew that she could make this house a home for them.

I know that this was all because of Kate's book. If we had not taken the steps that Kate suggested – emotional detachment, no longer looking at it as our home, and if we had not removed all the clutter, we would not have sold our house. Looking back now it has made it easier for us to move onto our next phase.

Thank you once again, Kate, for the huge impact you had on our lives.

Fiona and Jan Aucamp

Brigitte says: ***The energy of the house already feels lighter and the rooms feel more spacious and make it easier for me to let it go – with love.*** Clutter be gone – House be sold! That's my new mantra for helping me get my house from FOR SALE to SOLD smoothly and efficiently, to get me the best possible price and to find the most amazing new owners for my home. As with any project, getting started was the hardest part ... but with Kate nudging me along gently, I did it and I'm so grateful for Kate's incredible level-headedness and support.

The first few exercises brought up all kinds of weird emotions – remembering the initial excitement of owning a new home five years ago, to processing some tough events like my divorce and an armed robbery. Later exercises helped me to rediscover the forgotten good memories after all this time and to be left with a more balanced outlook in terms of the house, which makes it easier for me to let it go – with love. The energy of the house already feels lighter and the rooms feel more spacious. We've got a small amount of clutter clearing to do, but luckily that's next on the agenda ... Then there's a small list of things to attend to before the house is ready to go on the market – just in time for the perfect buyer to walk in and snap it up! It's really looking awesome – it's so lovely to be able to know *exactly* where everything is and to be able to locate things so easily.

Brigitte White

Debi says: *I definitely feel in me a complete shift of energy and lightness.* Firstly, thank you for sharing your amazing process with us. It has been a truly wonderful experience for my two daughters and me ... of interest to me was the parallel we shared regarding our most difficult times together in our home and what it has taught us. Each step really engaged a different feeling for us, and every one of the exercises was really meaningful. I also learned a few things weighing on my girls about our relocation, which I had been overlooking in terms of the emotional separation we are in fact all having. Mostly, I definitely feel in me a complete shift of energy and lightness. *Debi O'Brien*

Radia says: *Thank you for opening my eyes – I re-sold my house to ME! There's no denying it, Kate, your system works!* Let me explain ... I was just going through the motions of buying a house, no excitement, it was just a place to live in. I was miserable in this house for nine months since I bought it, and made up my mind to 'get rid of it'. Kate started me on her course. I could not believe that from Day 1, the emotions I had cropped up inside, that I first had to let go of, to recognize my house and what it meant to me. With clearing out the emotional attachment and physical clutter, my spirits lifted every day as I worked on the course. I changed my mindset about the house and, as it became cleaner and prettier, I fell in love with it for the first time.

Now, I feel like buying my own house. I am so in love with it. I want to thank you for opening my eyes, my heart and my mind. The course has made me stop and think, and do act. It has made me count my blessings, and appreciate what I have. I did not believe that cleaning a house would involve 'inner cleaning'.

Thank you - may you be blessed for your inspiration. *Radia Berry*

OTHER WORKS BY KATE:
CLEAR YOUR CLUTTER: ISBN 978-1-920479-68-8

A practical, no-nonsense book that teaches you the WHY and the HOW of ridding yourself of emotional, physical and body clutter.

Having helped thousands of clients with her unique program, Kate Emmerson, the Quick Shift Deva, now shares her enthusiasm for and expertise in clearing clutter at all levels with you. Her life and work motto is to LIVE LIGHT, LIVE LARGE and this book tells you how to follow suit. Let her inspire you with her in-depth understanding of the psychology of clutter and how it keeps you from living the life you are destined to live NOW.

Having helped thousands of clients with her unique program, Kate Emmerson, the Quick Shift Deva, now shares her enthusiasm for and expertise in clearing clutter at all levels with you. Her life and work motto is to LIVE LIGHT, LIVE LARGE and this book tells you how to follow suit. Let her inspire you with her in-depth understanding of the psychology of clutter and how it keeps you from living the life you are destined to live NOW.

- Understand the full spectrum of clutter through an empowering definition.
- Learn how the 3 aspects of clutter intertwine to hold each other hostage.
- Face up to the reality of your current clutter without shame or blame.
- Understand how clutter stops you from moving forward & LIVING LARGE.
- Face your personal sabotage system and why you really have clutter.
- Accurately calculate the monetary cost of your clutter.

- Practically shift your clutter following Kate's 28-day step-by-step process.
- Stay motivated to tackle the overwhelm associated with clutter.
- Learn simple tricks, tools and systems to stay in charge going forward.

Praise for Clear your clutter "This is the BEST book on clutter clearing I have ever read. ... Simply brilliant, brilliantly simple. I love it!" *Fiona Harrold* | AUTHOR, LIFE COACH

"Kate shares immediate, doable, straightforward tips on how to liberate your life and yourself from being controlled and restricted by too much stuff, around you and inside you!" *Dorianne Cara Weil* | "DR. D" RADIO TALK SHOW HOST

"The fantastic balance of useful information, anecdotes and straightforward easy to follow practical guidelines ensures the reader will follow the processes through to the end and achieve an enhanced life, as a result." *Dr. Colin La Grange*

"Kate's approachable, direct and conversational style is inviting and like a friend, she guides the reader through every phase, gently and sometimes firmly leading the way to a lighter and more expansive space." *Bonita Nuttall* | TV HOST AND KEYNOTE SPEAKER

"The bible says it's more blessed to give than to receive, yet we still find ourselves in a world obsessed with having 'more' – which makes Kate's no quibble approach to clutter, all the more refreshing - not to mention the practical proof that less is more." *Dr Michael Mol* | EXECUTIVE PRODUCER

"If you have ever had any kind of resistance to keeping your space exactly that, a space, then Kate's words will brightly and swiftly sweep you up. Her clarity and practical tools will liberate your body, mind, heart and house from what stops, blocks and hinders you in life." *Tiamara Williams* | PRESIDENT INSPIRING LIVES GLOBAL CHANGE MAKER, TV HOST, AUTHOR

DITCH YOUR GLITCH: ISBN 978-1-928201-62-5

A purposeful journey to face your "glitch". An honest process to *step in*, *step up* and *step out*.

Ditch your glitch is true to Kate's well-loved style of being honest, authentic, inspirational and compassionate. Her unique process of 'step in, step up and step out' into the world helps you shift gears exponentially to find a new way forward to shine your light. It's filled with snippets of her own fascinating life story and interwoven with success stories from brave clients who faced their glitch. This book takes you on a powerful yet practical journey to the self, through deep, inner exploration and transformation so that you can heed her call to live a life of magnificence.

- Discover five glitches and identify what's tripping you up.
- Follow 21 easy steps to get jiggy with your goals.
- Liberate yourself through the "potato" exercise.
- Take responsibility and finally stop the blame game.
- Ditch sabotaging self-limiting beliefs.
- Stop letting your fear be bigger than you.
- Set ballsy boundaries once and for all.
- Let go of emotional baggage to unleash energy.
- Boost your bucket before you kick the bucket.

Reviews of DITCH YOUR GLITCH

"Was I surprised when she went straight to my glitch at the beginning of the book, describing it in the finest detail. It made me pay attention to what followed. My thinking shifted in the most powerful way. Forever."

Melanie Brummer | ENTREPRENEUR, AUTHOR. SOUTH AFRICA

"Like a good friend who tells you hard truths, Kate takes you firmly by the hand and guides you on a challenging, life-changing journey. Bravely revealing her own story throughout, she gives you the courage to face your glitches and heal past hurts ... with the take-charge tools you need to transform your life."

Fiona Davern, EXECUTIVE EDITOR DESTINY MAGAZINE.

"A step-by-step process beyond your comfort zone to honestly face aspects of yourself and your life that you may not be comfortable with and to realize that success in your life starts with you. This book will challenge you to get started on a whole new path to success and fulfillment with a renewed zest. I know that's what it did for me." *Colleen Larsen* | CE: BUSINESS ENGAGE

"This book is a revolutionary eye opener into where I am right now, what needs to be addressed, how to shift change and, more importantly, how to ensure a continuity of growth." *Janine Starkey* | HOUSE OF JANINE

"*Ditch your Glitch* encourages us to look deep into our core to find our magnificence...she doesn't just talk the talk; she walks the walk." *Carol Scibelli* | AUTHOR. New York

"A book that you won't be able to put down! It truly will help you shift your life and perspective ... will inspire you to take action today! Kate's book will help you to reach unlimited potential!" *Beth Bracaglia* | CHIEF SIMPLICITY OFFICER OF SIMPLY ORGANIZED, ELLICOTT CITY

"Kate doesn't tell you how to do it – she shows you. By using her own personal journey as insightful examples, she makes you feel as if she is there with you in this easy to follow, actionable, transformative and very readable book." *Tessa Graham* | CAPTURING BRILLIANCE, CREATING BRANDS, BUILDING BUSINESSES

"A truly inspiring book that helped me finally get over my issues with forgiving, which was the hardest part. I am now in control of my emotions and I will not allow people to use and abuse me anymore. I will buy this book for all my family members and friends who I know will benefit from it." *Yolanda Duvenhage* | A BRAVE WOMAN RECLAIMING HER LIFE

THE SECRETS OF THE KEYS - TRANSFORMATIONAL MOVIE
I had the privilege of appearing as an expert in a USA produced film, which has since won 2 awards!

What if your doctor told you you're going to die? That's exactly what happens to motivational speaker and author Elizabeth, the main character in *The Secrets of the Keys*. Throughout her career, she's been guiding others, and she has to tap into that same inspiration to make sense of her situation.

Then she finds her own spiritual guide, Gwen, who has an intriguing opportunity for her. Gwen takes Elizabeth on a mystical journey where they meet a range of impressive experts who are eager for her to accept Gwen's unique offer of a new kind of existence.

It's an empowering and transformational film that is both entertaining and beautiful. It will forever change the way you look at life.

It's written and produced by Robin Jay, who has a unique hybrid style of creating a fictional story, to which she adds some of the most respected experts in the field of personal development, including me!

This is what Robin said: "Kate's insights for de-cluttering our lives so that we can move forward and experience greater joy every day is a message that everyone needs to hear. She's an absolute genius! I know her message will have viewers rushing to declutter their homes, as well as rid themselves of their useless emotions and all the other 'baggage' that has been weighing them down."

The Secrets of the Keys stars these outstanding experts:
- Brian Tracy, international business and success guru
- Rev Michael B. Beckwith, spiritual leader and founder of AGAPE International Spiritual Center
- John Assaraf, spiritual entrepreneur, philanthropist and teacher

- Dannion Brinkley, author of *Saved by the Light* and founder of *The Twilight Brigade*
- Don Miguel Ruiz, author of *The Four Agreements*
- Gloria Loring, singer, songwriter and actress This remarkable film also features these experts from around the world:
- Kate Emmerson – International speaker, author and coach.
- Dr. Alfredo Besosa, founder and director of the Mind/Body/Spirit International Institute in Bogota, Colombia.
- Carol Scibelli, speaker, writer and author of *Poor Widow Me*
- Dr. Terry Gordon, cardiologist (retired), American Heart Association National Physician of the Year and author of *No Storm Lasts Forever*
- William Liu, life coach and transformational leader
- Leslie Stein, one of the first women to attend West Point Military Academy in the USA, author of *Penny Perspectives*
- Farida Akadiri, life coach and self-proclaimed "Queen of Manifestation"
- Carly Alyssa Thorne, Multi-sensory, Multi-media Transformation Muse, Author, Filmmaker To order your copies of this inspirational film, go to the shop page on my website: www.kate-emmerson.com.

Until we meet again, I wish you courage and boldness on your path to LIVE LIGHTER, LIVE LARGER!

With lightness,
Kate

CPSIA information can be obtained
at www.ICGtesting.com
Printed in the USA
BVHW032150200121
598296BV00013B/76